Dining
in
HISTORIC
KENTUCKY

A Restaurant Guide With Recipes

by Marty Godbey

Illustrations by James Asher

McClanahan
Publishing House

Copyright © 1985, by Marty Godbey
Illustrations © McClanahan Publishing House

All rights reserved. No part of this book
may be copied or reproduced without permission from
the publisher, except by a reviewer who may quote brief
passages in a review.

Library of Congress Catalog Card Number: 85–61512
International Standard Book Number: 0–913383–04–X $12.95

Cover photograph: Elmwood Inn, Perryville, Kentucky

Illustrations by James Asher
Cover photographs by James Archambeault
Cover design by James Asher
Manufactured in the United States of America

All book order correspondence should be addressed to:
McClanahan Publishing House, Incorporated
Rt. 2, Box 32
Kuttawa, Kentucky 42055
(502) 388–9388

INTRODUCTION

KENTUCKY'S TALENT FOR hospitality is renowned: from the time when a frontier traveler in the wilderness was welcomed to a crossroads tavern, great pride has been taken in the foods offered to guests. Even under conditions of poverty, the best the house has to offer is set forth; in times of plenty, polished walnut and cherry tables reflect silver laden with delicacies, and visitors are pressed to indulge themselves.

The finest of locally available ingredients has always been used here, whether wild mint is blended with a beverage made of limestone water and homegrown corn, or mahogany-colored "old" ham is sandwiched in crisp beaten biscuits, or tender young chickens are fried golden brown. A tradition of good food carefully prepared and graciously served has been carried on for generations.

To Kentuckians, history is as much a part of daily life as is food—roads and buildings known by Daniel Boone, George Rogers Clark, and Abraham Lincoln not only remain, they are frequently still in use, cherished for their indirect contribution to the Commonwealth and the Nation.

A few of the establishments that provided food and lodging for these and other early Kentuckians are still in business; many other buildings of historic significance have been restored or refurbished and converted into restaurants. These were constructed as blacksmith shops, schools, simple farmsteads or opulent city residences; and some have had several "lives," not always respectable.

There are no two alike, and because they belong to people who value the past enough to utilize old buildings, with the attendant inconveniences, they are all very special places.

Although the buildings are old, the food reflects current tastes and interests. Kentucky fare today is more diversified than might be suspected—traditional regional favorites are joined by innovative methods of preparation and products new to the area. Ready availability of fresh seafoods has been an important influence, as has an awareness of diet and nutrition in today's restaurant-goers. And Kentucky's ethnic mix has contributed such delights as hot German slaw, antipasto, gumbo, and stuffed cabbage to an already rich and varied list.

A visit to any of Kentucky's restaurants in historic buildings is well repaid, for an appreciation of the past is as easily absorbed as the excellent food, and the diner leaves satisfied in more ways than one.

Dining in Historic Kentucky
as a Travel Guide

A LIST OF NEARLY TWO hundred restaurants in historic buildings in Kentucky was accumulated from advertisements, old travel books, word-of-mouth reports, and personal experience. Each restaurant was investigated, and those selected for *Dining In Historic Kentucky* were chosen on a basis of historic, architectural, or culinary interest (frequently all three) coupled with business stability.

The author, often with companions, ate anonymously in every restaurant included, to ensure the same treatment any hungry traveler might receive, and found friendly, courteous service as well as good food.

Those unfamiliar with Kentucky should be advised that there are many counties in which alcoholic beverages may not legally be sold. If beverages are available, it will be so noted in the resource information about each restaurant.

Symbols used for brevity include charge card references: AE= American Express, CB= Carte Blanche, DC= Diner's Club, MC= Master Card, V= Visa.

Most of these restaurants would fall into the "moderate" category of expensiveness; an effort was made to include all price ranges, and special prices for children are indicated where offered. Using entrée prices as a gauge, dollar signs ($) are used to indicate reasonable ($), moderate ($$), and more expensive ($$$). The amount of money spent in any restaurant is increased by the "extras" ordered, i.e., appetizers, drinks, and side orders.

In traditional Southern service, main dishes are frequently accompanied by vegetable(s), salad, and dessert, and in these cases, the price is counted as an entrée price.

None of these restaurants would be considered expensive by East or West Coast standards; if cost is a determining factor, however, most restaurants will gladly provide a price range over the telephone.

Visitors are cautioned that although some of the restaurants included in *Dining in Historic Kentucky* are well off the beaten track, they may have enthusiastic popularity, and busy seasons are determined by such events as The Kentucky Derby (first Saturday in May) not familiar to non-residents. To avoid disappointment, CALL AHEAD FOR RESERVATIONS.

Contents

What a great combination -- good food served in historic places! In Kentucky, we savor both our fine cuisine and our important past, and we enjoy sharing them with people from all over the country and the world.

The restaurants described in this book are as diverse as the Commonwealth itself. From the mountains in the east to the lake country in the west, our guests may step across a new threshold in dining, cooking, and cultural tradition with every turn of the page.

Kentuckians are proud of their history, traditions, and the contributions our people have made to the cultural and economic development of this great nation. With its fascinating account of historic buildings and varied assortment of recipes, this is not only a guidebook to good eating, but it is also a tribute to our very special place in history.

Each place described in these pages has its own story to tell, and coupled with the superior cuisine, you will find the finest in southern hospitality as well. Welcome to the land of Boone, Lincoln, and Jefferson Davis, and happy eating upon the table tops of history!

Sincerely,

Martha Layne Collins

AN EQUAL OPPORTUNITY EMPLOYER M/F/H

KENTUCKY

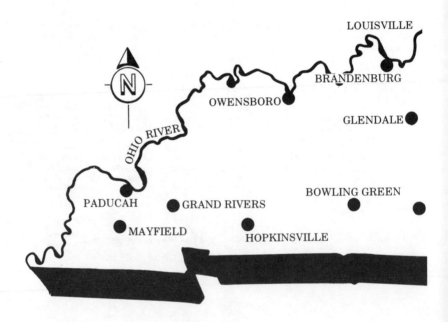

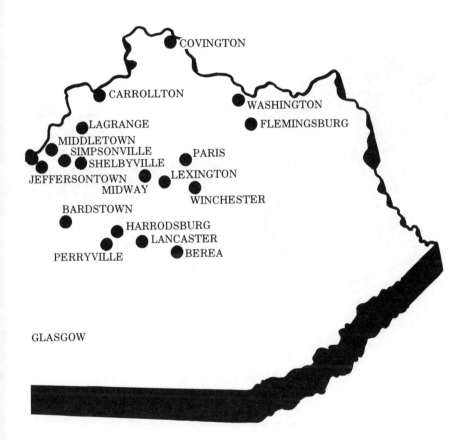

COVINGTON

CARROLLTON

WASHINGTON

LAGRANGE

FLEMINGSBURG

MIDDLETOWN
SIMPSONVILLE

PARIS

SHELBYVILLE

JEFFERSONTOWN

LEXINGTON

MIDWAY

WINCHESTER

BARDSTOWN

HARRODSBURG

LANCASTER

PERRYVILLE

BEREA

GLASGOW

THE DEPOT
Flemingsburg

THE COMMONWEALTH OF

Kentucky began as Kentucky County, Virginia; it was divided into Fayette, Lincoln, and Jefferson counties in 1780, and by 1792, when Kentucky became a separate state, subdivided into nine counties. The state was split into smaller and smaller counties, as many rural Kentuckians believed the size of a county should allow any citizen to ride to the county seat and return home the same day.

The county court was essential to the business of nearly everyone, and Court Monday, scheduled by a statute enacted by the General Assembly, occurred on a specified Monday of the month in each county. Hundreds of people attended Court Day, not only for court transactions, but to trade horses, dogs, guns, and other pioneer necessities. Peddlers traveled from one county seat to another, timing their arrival with the Court Day crowds.

Autumn Court Days gave farmers an opportunity to sell their harvest and a chance to visit neighbors before bad weather. In a few towns, the custom of a fall Court Day still stands, and Maysville, Mount Sterling, and Flemingsburg each hold an entire weekend of festivities in conjunction with their Court Days. Streets turn into open markets, with booths of antiques, regional foods, entertainment, and flea market items of every kind. People come from many surrounding counties to participate, as court activities are now a minor part of the proceedings.

Court Day in Flemingsburg is the first weekend in October.

The Depot Restaurant in Flemingsburg occupies a charming structure that was erected about 1910 to service a narrow-gauge line connecting Flemingsburg with the Louisville and Nashville Railroad. Chartered in 1870 as the Covington, Flemingsburg and Pound Gap Railway, the 17-mile line was operated under numerous names and partnerships during its 79 years of existance. The last train ran December 6, 1955.

The building, a Kentucky Landmark, was opened as a restaurant in 1984, and maintains a comfortable waiting-room feeling. Fresh and clean in its gray paint, The Depot offers home cooked meals, breakfast any time, and a Saturday night all-you-can-eat fish special. Other evening specials include

Prime Rib (Friday) and Barbecued Beef Ribs (Thursday), with regular dinner items of steaks, country ham, and turkey and dressing. A generous salad bar is always available, as are sandwich platters, omelets, and hot weather treats of country ham salad, fruit plates, and chicken salad plates. Manager Paulette Holt's homemade soups are winter favorites, and an old-fashioned Hot Apple Dumpling is a great end to an excursion to Flemingsburg.

The Depot, P.O. Box 107, Flemingsburg, Kentucky, 41041, is on Electric Avenue, and is open Monday through Saturday from 6 a.m. to 10 p.m., and on Sunday from 7 a.m. to 8 p.m., with continuous service. (606)845-0706. Dress is casual, reservations are accepted but not necessary, and there is a children's menu; Tuesday is "Kiddie Day," when those under ten years eat free. MC, V. ($)

THE DEPOT FRIED BANANA PEPPERS

**Whole banana peppers,
canned in water, or
fresh, raw
1 egg, lightly beaten**

**1 to 2 Tablespoons milk
Flour for dredging
Salt and black pepper
Deep fat for frying**

Split peppers lengthwise. In shallow bowl, beat egg with milk; dip peppers in egg/milk mixture, dredge with flour, seasoned with salt and pepper, then dip again in egg, then flour. Fry in deep fat at 360 degrees until golden brown. Serve at once.
Note: the same ingredients and method may be used to fry zucchini cauliflower, cucumbers, or green peppers.

THE DEPOT CABBAGE PUDDING

**1 head cabbage
Salt
½ pound American cheese,
shredded**

**¼ pound saltine crackers,
crumbled
1 cup milk
¼ pound butter, melted**

Cut cabbage into bite-sized pieces, place in saucepan with salted water to cover, and cook until just tender. Do not overcook. Drain all water, reserving one cup.

Place cooked cabbage and reserved cooking liquid into casserole. Mix in cheese and coarsely crumbled crackers. Add milk and butter, and bake at 350 degrees about 30 minutes or until golden brown and bubbling. Serves eight to ten. Note: chopped broccoli may be substituted for cabbage.

THE DEPOT BISCUITS

2 cups self-rising flour
1 cup milk
6 Tablespoons vegetable oil

About ½ cup additional flour

In large mixing bowl, place 2 cups flour with milk and vegetable oil. Mix into a thick batter with a spoon, then add ½ cup flour or less, and work into a ball of dough.

Turn out onto floured board and roll about ½-inch thick. Cut into 2½-inch rounds, place on greased baking sheet, and grease top of each biscuit with oil. Bake at 425 to 450 degrees until brown and crusty on top. Yields about one dozen large biscuits.

BRODRICK'S TAVERN
Washington

KENTUCKY'S EARLY

travelers, rafting down the Ohio from Pennsylvania and the Northeast, often disembarked at a landing called Limestone. Many of them dismantled their flatboats, loaded the timbers onto wagons and struggled up the steep hill to the little settlement of Washington.

The four-mile journey took an entire day, but the road was wide and smooth, trampled through the canebrake by herds of buffalo on their way to salt springs. Tired pioneers were glad to stop for the night, and many of them settled in the prospering village, so that by 1790, Washington was the second largest town in Kentucky, with 119 log houses and 462 people. In that same year, a tavern license was granted to David Brodrick.

Much of Washington remains—it has changed little in 150 years—and the entire village was placed on the National Register of Historic Places in 1970.

Interesting shops occupy many of the 18th- and 19th-century buildings, and seven historic structures are open to the public, depending upon weather and demand, including the Simon Kenton Shrine, the birthplace of Confederate General Albert Sidney Johnston and a cabin built from the flatboat on which a family of 15 traveled down the Ohio in 1787.

Guided tours of the village are available on summer weekends and during the Frontier Christmas celebration (the first weekend in December), and a self-guided walking tour is possible any time with a free map from the Tourist Center.

Once again, hungry people flock to Brodrick's Tavern, owned by the Mason County Historical Society, and a restaurant since 1973. During years as a residence, the building was enlarged, almost doubling the original size, but original woodwork in the entry hall has been preserved, as has the original tavern license. The 1870's addition, to the right of the door, adds space to seat the many visitors who appreciate the generous buffet and reasonable prices of restaurant owners Coburn and Susan Davidson.

Known for "good country cooking," Brodrick's offers steaks, chicken, seafood, pork, and ham dinners, sandwiches, and a selection of soups and salads served buffet style. The Thanksgiving feast is often served to 1500 people during the day, many of whom drive great distances to participate.

David Brodrick would be pleased.

Brodrick's Tavern, Washington, Kentucky 41096, is open daily, 11 a.m. to 8:30 p.m. winter weekdays, to 9:30 weekends, and 11 a.m. to 9 p.m. summer weekdays, to 9:30 weekends, with continuous serving. It is closed the first week in January. (606)759-7934. Washington is four miles south of Maysville, about 50 miles northeast of Lexington, just off U.S. 68. Dress is casual, and no reservations and no charge cards are accepted. ($)

BRODRICK'S TAVERN SCALLOPED OYSTERS

3 pints oysters, drained, reserving
1 ¾ cup oyster liquor
6 cups medium coarse cracker crumbs
1 ½ cups (3 sticks) butter or margarine, melted

1 ½ teaspoons salt
3 dashes white pepper
2 ½ cups cream or half and half
¾ teaspoon Worces tershire sauce

Combine crumbs, butter, salt, and pepper. Spread ⅓ of the crumbs in a large, shallow, buttered pan; cover with ½ of the oysters. Top with second layer of crumbs and remaining oysters. Combine cream, oyster liquor, and Worcestershire sauce and pour over oysters. Top with remaining crumbs. Bake at 350 degrees 50 minutes to 1 hour, until crisp and browned. Serves 12.

BRODRICK'S TAVERN HOMEMADE DUMPLINGS

2 cups flour
1 teaspoon salt
3 teaspoons baking powder

1 cup milk
4 Tablespoons melted fat or salad oil

Sift dry ingredients, add milk and oil to make soft dough. Drop dumplings by tablespoon into boiling broth, cover tightly, and steam without lifting cover for 12 to 15 minutes. Serves eight to ten.

BRODRICK'S TAVERN FRUIT SALAD

3 large sweet apples
3 bananas
Juice of one lemon
One 16-ounce can apricots
One 16-ounce can peaches
One 16-ounce can
   pineapple

One 16-ounce bag
miniature
marshmallows
Two 5-ounce boxes instant
   vanilla pudding mix

Cut up apples and slice banannas; sprinkle with lemon juice to keep from darkening. Drain canned fruit, reserving juice. Use this juice instead of milk to make pudding, according to directions on package. If juice is insufficient, add water to the right amount. Cut canned fruit into bite-size pieces, and add all fruit to mixed pudding. Chill until glazed. Serves 12.

BRODRICK'S TAVERN TRANSPARENT PIE

One 9 or 10-inch unbaked
   pie shell
3 Tablespoons flour
1 cup sugar
1 cup light brown sugar

3 eggs
½ cup cream
Salt
½ cup butter, melted
1 teaspoon vanilla

Combine flour and sugars; beat in eggs, cream, salt, butter, and vanilla. Pour into pie shell and bake at 425 degrees for 30 to 35 minutes, or until firm. Serves eight.

HIGH COURT INN
Winchester

Iɴ ᴀɴ ᴀɢᴇ ᴡʜᴇɴ ʙᴜs-
iness establishments have rushed to the-new-mall-out-on-the-
highway, downtown Winchester is not only refreshing, it is
a reminder of what most small towns COULD be. A recent
downtown revitalization project has encouraged painting and
refurbishing of the charming Victorian buildings, and shops
and offices are as busy and prosperous as ever.

High Court Inn opened in December of 1982, and occupies
a building that, as early as 1886, housed a saloon and pool
hall, with the saloonkeeper's family residing upstairs. Now,
there is a dentist's office below, and the second-floor restaurant is entered by an obscure street door to one side.

Passing down a narrow hall and up a steep staircase, both
with a distinctly 19th century feeling, the first-time visitor
is unprepared for what awaits upstairs. Small rooms have
been swept into one large room, bright and spacious, with
curving expanses of plaster to delineate seating areas. Delicate Victorian fireplaces remain for coziness, hoop-back Wind-
sor chairs are grouped around tables of varying sizes, and
stark white walls provide a gallery for works by local artist
Holly VanMeter.

High Court Inn's tall windows overlook the spectacular
Clark County Courthouse, from which the restaurant derived
its name. This imposing ediface, on the National Register
of Historic Places, was built in the 1850's, and has been remodeled and expanded several times without changing its original
Greek Revival character. It is the focus of downtown Winchester, and residents are justifiably proud of it.

Bill and Karen Espy, owners of High Court Inn, are equally
proud of their establishment; all foods are natural, fresh, and
prepared entirely by hand. "The only chemical in the kitchen
is soap," boasts Chef/host Bill, who does not even use a food
processor in his solicitude to stay in touch with his creations.

The menu has a Kentucky flavor, with beef, seafood,
chicken and stuffed broiled catfish predominating; steaks, cut
by hand, are a specialty, as are several house sauces. Vegetables are particularly good, fresh and crisp, and the custardy
corn pudding is most unusual and delicious. At lunch, there
is a wide choice of salads, sandwiches, and lighter fare, and

at both meals, homemade hot breads (especially the whole wheat loaf) and the homemade cheesecake are most enjoyable.

High Court Inn, 27 South Main Street, Winchester, Kentucky 40391, is open from 11 a.m. to 10 p.m., Monday through Thursday, and until 10:30 p.m. Friday and Saturday, with meals served continuously. (606)745-4863. Winchester is about 15 miles east of Lexington, via I-64 or US 60. Dress is informal, all beverages are served, and reservations are available but not necessary. AE, MC, V. ($$)

HIGH COURT INN HOUSE DRESSING

3 eggs
3 ounces Grey Poupon
  (Dijon) mustard
1 Tablespoon granulated
  garlic
1 teaspoon white pepper
1 teaspoon salt

1 Tablespoon
  Worcestershire sauce
10 ounces salad oil
2 Tablespoons Parmesan
  cheese, grated
3 ounces tarragon vinegar

Mix all ingredients except vinegar to a mayonnaise texture, using a wire whip for best results. Blend in vinegar. Serves eight to ten.

HIGH COURT INN CHICKEN OSCAR

Eight 5 to 6 ounce chicken
  breasts, boned
1 pound broccoli,
  parboiled until crisp
1 cup cooked rice
1 small onion, finely
  chopped

4 ounces (1 stick) butter
3 chicken bouillon cubes
24 shrimp, boiled, shelled,
  and deveined
Sauce (see below)
Lemon slices for garnish

Sauté chicken breasts about 4 minutes, or until done; set aside. Melt butter in saucepan, add onion and bouillon cubes. Stir until dissolved, and mix into cooked rice. Divide broccoli onto 8 ovenproof plates; spoon rice over broccoli. Place chicken breasts on rice, top with 3 shrimp and 2 ounces of sauce. Broil 3-4 minutes or bake at 325 or 350 degrees for 10 to 15 minutes, or until sauce bubbles. Garnish with lemon and serve. Serves eight.

Sauce:

2 cups milk	2 ounces (½ stick) butter
6 ounces flat beer	¼ cup flour
1 teaspoon granulated garlic	3 ounces Cheddar cheese, grated
1 teaspoon white pepper	2 tablespoons Parmesan cheese, grated
1 teaspoon paprika	
1 cup chicken stock	

Bring first six ingredients to slow boil, being careful not to scorch. Rub butter and flour together until smooth, and add to boiling mixture with cheeses. Blend together until smooth and creamy.

HIGH COURT INN CHEESECAKE

One 9-inch graham cracker crust	3 whole eggs
1 pound cream cheese, at room temperature	1 teaspoon vanilla
1 cup sugar	Juice and zest of ½ lemon
	Topping (see below for recipe)

Whip cream cheese with sugar until smooth; add eggs, vanilla, lemon juice and zest, and mix at low speed for 2 minutes. Low speed is a MUST to avoid air bubbles. Pour into graham cracker crust and bake at 300 degrees for 40 to 60 minutes, or until firm. Cool for 30 minutes before adding topping. Serves ten.

Topping:

8 ounces sour cream	1 ½ teaspoons sugar
1 teaspoon Vanilla	

Blend all ingredients. Pour over baked cake and bake at 300 degrees for 10 minutes. Allow to cool for one hour.
Note: to vary flavor, omit lemon and add chocolate chips or strawberries, etc.

DUNCAN TAVERN
Paris

WHEN MAJOR JOSEPH

Duncan built his imposing stone tavern in 1788, he had an eye to the future: his elegant 3-story building contained 20 rooms, although surrounding buildings, including the Bourbon County Courthouse, were simple log structures. A ballroom, billiard room, and basement barroom are mentioned in early writing, and handsome original woodwork, blue ash floors, doors and their intricate locks remain as examples of the fine craftsmanship employed. Among early visitors were Daniel Boone, Simon Kenton, Colonel James Smith, and Governor James Garrard.

Left a young widow with six children, Anne Duncan built an adjacent house about 1803 in which to live, and leased the tavern, which operated for over 150 years under various names. In 1940, Duncan Tavern was deeded to the Kentucky Society, Daughters of the American Revolution, who restored and furnished it as their state shrine. The Anne Duncan House was acquired in 1955, and its restoration incorporated fine cabinetwork from many historic Kentucky buildings which had been demolished.

Today, the two buildings, Kentucky Landmarks placed on the National Register in 1973, are open to the public for tours. On view are mementoes of famous early Kentuckians, and a collection of fine antique Kentucky furniture donated by D.A.R. members and friends. In the former tavern basement, The John Fox, Jr. Library, dedicated to the beloved Kentucky author of "The Little Shepherd of Kingdom Come," houses a historical and genealogical library which is available for use.

Meals are no longer served on a regular basis at Duncan Tavern, but it is a famous catering center, and groups of 20 or more may schedule meals, receptions, or parties by appointment. Alma Stapleton, in charge of Duncan Tavern's food since 1976, describes it as "A gracious old place to have a party," and party food is her main enthusiasm. Aided by her son, David O'Neill, and her grandaughter, Dana Gulley, Mrs. Stapleton serves brunch, coffee, luncheon, tea, and dinner, often preparing two or three parties a day.

Party food for a reception might be spiced tea, finger sandwiches, pecan tassies and petit fours, plus dips with fresh vegetables, little quiches, fresh fruit dipped in chocolate, and puff paste filled with chicken salad. Luncheon or dinner entrées of chicken, ham, or prime rib are accompanied by vegetable casseroles, corn soufflé, yeast rolls or strawberry bread, something unexpected and delicious, and the popular Schaum Torte.

Duncan Tavern, 323 High Street, Paris, Kentucky, 40361, is open for tours Tuesday through Saturday, from 10 a.m. to 12 Noon, and from 1 to 4 p.m., and on Sunday from 1:30 to 4 p.m. The library is open during the same hours. (606)987-1788. Meals are served only to groups of 20 or more by prior arrangement, usually several months in advance, and price is determined by the menu. No charge cards; personal checks accepted. Tour cost is $1.50 for adults, $.80 for children; library use is $2.00 a day.

DUNCAN TAVERN CRÈME DE VOLAILLE*

4 or 5 pound chicken (hen preferred), boiled
1 cup canned mushrooms
3 Tablespoons butter
3 Tablespoons flour
1 pint milk, part cream for flavor

3 eggs
Salt and red or white pepper
Chopped parsley
Grated onion or onion juice

Remove chicken meat from bones, discarding skin, and grind meat with mushrooms. In saucepan, blend butter and flour over low heat, add creamy milk, and cook until thickened. Add this with eggs to chicken mixture, and beat well. Season with remaining ingredients and pour into greased mold. Cover with 4 layers of waxed paper and tie down tightly. Place mold in pan of hot water and steam in oven 1 ½ hours at 325 degrees. Serve with a cream or mushroom sauce.

DUNCAN TAVERN "CAN'T FAIL" MERINGUES*

1 pound confectioner's sugar
6 egg whites, unbeaten

1 teaspoon cream of tartar
1 ½ teaspoons vanilla

In mixer bowl, beat sugar and egg whites together for 10

minutes at high speed. Add cream of tartar and beat 10 minutes more. Add vanilla. Drop on waxed paper on cookie sheet, and bake at 250 degrees for 20 minutes. Increase temperature to 275 degrees and bake 20 minutes more.

DUNCAN TAVERN SPOON BREAD

3 cups milk
3 eggs, beaten
1 cup white cornmeal,
(stone ground, if
possible)

3 teaspoons baking powder
1 teaspoon salt
3 teaspoons sugar
2 Tablespoons butter

In saucepan, stir meal into 2 cups milk, and boil over medium heat until mushy. Add remaining milk with other ingredients and pour into greased oven-proof dish. Bake at 350 degrees for 30 minutes, or until browned. Serve at once from dish.

DUNCAN TAVERN SCHAUM TORTE

6 egg whites (reserve yolks
for another use)
2 cups sugar
1 teaspoon baking powder
16 ounces whipped
topping, thawed, OR

2 cups whipped cream
16 ounces frozen
strawberries, thawed

Beat eggs with baking powder until very stiff, adding sugar a little at a time. Spread in 9 × 13 pan (do not grease) and bake at 275 degrees for one hour. Remove from oven. Using spatula, remove top crust at once and set aside; it will be in small pieces. Cool. Mix topping or whipped cream and strawberries, with their juice, and spread on bottom crust of torte in the pan. Replace pieces of top crust, fitting together to cover strawberry mixture. Refrigerate six or seven hours, and cut into 15 or 18 squares to serve.

* from KENTUCKY D.A.R. COOKBOOK. Paris, Kentucky. Copyright © 1970. Used by permission.

BOONE TAVERN
Berea

Berea College, In The

quaint little community "Where the Bluegrass meets the mountains," began in 1855 as a tiny non-sectarian and inter-racial school for needy Appalachian children. Today, 1500 students, 80 per cent of them from the Southern Appalachians, benefit from Berea's unique work-study program.

Every student works at least 10 hours a week while carrying a full academic load, defraying all or part of board, room, and health fees. Tuition is guaranteed, supported by endowment and gifts. Berea Student Industries are a source of income for the college, and the high-quality student crafts are available in college shops and through catalog sales.

In addition to working in woodcraft, wrought iron, weaving, lapidary, needlecraft, broomcraft and ceramics, students provide service in the college stores, farms, and laundry. About 150 of them, many studying hotel management, work in the Boone Tavern Hotel and Dining room. They wait tables, man the reception desk, work as bellhops and bookkeepers, and apprentice in the kitchen. Their eager-to-please service and bright young faces have helped to attract an ever-growing clientele, many of whom return year after year.

Boone Tavern was opened in 1909 as a 25-room guest house for the college, and rapidly became a popular stopover. Expanded in 1928, the three-story Georgian-style building covers most of a city block, with 57 overnight rooms, meeting rooms and a spacious lobby. Antique reproduction furniture throughout the hotel is from Student Industries. The dining room has many-paned windows overlooking the campus, and the overall atmosphere is one of homelike comfort.

Richard T. Hougen, Manager of Boone Tavern from 1940 to 1976, established and was head of the Hotel Management Department at Berea College. During his tenure he wrote three cookbooks which formed the basis for Boone Tavern's famed food, an updated Southern cuisine. His recipes are still used by the staff he trained, and the books are available in the lobby.

Fresh regional foods, often purchased from local farmers, are cleverly seasoned and attractively presented. Mountain

31

brook trout, lamb, chicken, pork chops, beef, and turkey are typical selections, and each meal comes with appetizer, salad, entrée, fresh vegetables and dessert, plus relishes at dinner. Two wonderful hot breads are passed at each meal (the spoon-bread, served only at dinner, is legendary); for dessert, rich Jefferson Davis Pie and Black Forest Cake contrast with Grapefruit Sherbet and Island Coconut Ice Cream.

Boone Tavern, Berea, Kentucky 40404, is open Monday through Saturday for breakfast from 7 to 9 a.m., for lunch 11:30 a.m. to 1:30 p.m., and for dinner 6 to 7:30 p.m. Sundays and holidays, breakfast is 7 to 9 a.m., lunch 12 Noon to 2 p.m., and dinner 6 to 7:30 p.m. (606)986-9358. Berea is 40 miles south of Lexington, just east of I-75. Dress code requires coats for men, dresses or tailored trousers for women, and reservations are requested; they are essential for weekends in April and October. There is a strict no-tipping policy. AE, D, MC, V. ($$)

BOONE TAVERN TEA GARDEN SALAD*

One 3-ounce package orange gelatin
1 cup hot, freshly made black tea
1 cup juice drained from oranges and pineapple

One 9-ounce can mandarin oranges, drained
One 9-ounce can crushed pineapple, drained
One 5-ounce can water chestnuts, drained

Dissolve gelatin in hot tea. Add juice from oranges and pineapple, with regular orange juice to fill the cup, if needed. Stir. Refrigerate until thickened. Cut water chestnuts into small slices, and add to gelatin with pineapple and oranges. Spoon mixture into 8 well-oiled molds and refrigerate until set. Unmold and serve with the following dressing. Serves eight.

Dressing:
1 cup whipped cream
½ cup mayonnaise

Grated rind of one orange
Pinch of mace

Mix together all ingredients; serve on top of salad.

BOONE TAVERN HEARTS OF ARTICHOKES FONDUE*

One 10-ounce package
frozen artichokes
1 cup cream sauce (see
below)
½ cup Swiss cheese, cut in
small pieces

½ cup bread crumbs,
mixed with
2 Tablespoons melted
butter
Dash of poultry seasoning

In saucepan, place artichoke hearts with 1 cup water and ½ teaspoon salt. Cover and bring to a boil. Remove from heat and allow to stand, covered, 15 minutes. Drain and place artichoke hearts in buttered casserole. Cover with cream sauce, dot on cheese, then top with bread crumbs. Sprinkle with poultry seasoning. Bake at 350 degrees for 30 minutes. Serves four.

Note: a medium cream sauce may be made of 1 ½ tablespoons flour, 1 ½ tablespoons butter, and 1 cup hot milk, cooked together over medium heat until thickened.

BOONE TAVERN JEFFERSON DAVIS PIE*

One 9-inch unbaked pie
shell
2 cups brown sugar
1 Tablespoon sifted flour
½ teaspoon nutmeg
1 cup cream

4 eggs, slightly beaten
1 teaspoon lemon juice
½ teaspoon grated lemon
rind
¼ cup melted margarine
Whipped cream for garnish

Sift sugar with flour and nutmeg; add cream and mix well. Add eggs, mix well, then add lemon juice, rind, and margarine. Beat well. Pour into pie shell and bake at 375 degrees for 45 minutes. Cool and serve with whipped cream. Serves eight.

* from COOKING WITH HOUGEN. Copyright © 1960 Richard T. Hougen, Berea, Kentucky. Used by permission.

THE MIKE FINK
Covington

KENTUCKY'S NORTHERN-

most and perhaps most unusual historic restaurant is a stern-wheeler tow boat permanently moored on the Kentucky shore of the Ohio River, near the mouth of the Licking River. This "Point" was known to navigators before 1751, and played an important part in Kentucky's early history.

The Mike Fink had an illustrious working career—one of the last of its kind to be constructed (in 1926), it towed oil barges under the name "John W. Hubbard." In the late 1940's, as "The Charles Dorrance," the cargo changed to coal, and it pushed the longest tow of its day on the Ohio River. The vessel became a restaurant in 1968, renamed for the roistering 19th-century keel-boatsman whose legendary exploits made him the riverboat version of Paul Bunyan.

Placed on the National Register in 1982, The Mike Fink has a restored exterior, even to the center-cut oak paddle-wheel, but the inside has been ingeniously remodeled to accommodate the restaurant's enormous clientele. Former coal storage areas house the kitchens, lower-level boiler rooms now hold refrigerators and food storage, and cabins for 25 passengers have been converted to a banquet room.

The visitor, traversing a gangplank that adapts to the level of the ever-changing river, enters a spacious dining room, which recaptures the romance and elegance of the riverboat era. Velvet upholstery, glass panels etched with famous riverboats, shining brass and polished oak add to comfort and atmosphere.

One of the most noticeable features of the room is the "Raw Bar," a riverboat institution, with iced shrimp, oysters, clams, stone crab claws and Alaska king crab legs piled high, waiting to become appetizers or whole meals for seafood lovers. Another is the Captain's Galley, where certain entrées are prepared for the visual and olfactory delight of anyone at hand.

"The Barge" is permanently alongside for additional seating, and offers spectacular views of The Ohio River and the Cincinnati skyline. Its glass walls open to river breezes in warm weather, making it a favorite seating location.

Under the direction of owner Ben Bernstein, food on The Mike Fink has a New Orleans flavor, with seafood and beef entrées predominating; giant burgers and sandwiches are added at lunch, and captains concoct such entrées as Steak Diane, Halibut Natchez, and Sautéed Seafood Supreme at tableside in the evening. Mississippi Bean Soup, New Orleans Bread Pudding, and other riverboat specialties are always on the menu.

The Mike Fink is more than a riverboat that serves food; it is a fine restaurant that happens to be on a riverboat.

The Mike Fink, at the foot of Greenup Street, Covington, Kentucky 41011, is open 11 a.m. to 12 Midnight Monday through Thursday, 11 a.m. to 1 a.m. Friday and Saturday, and 2 to 10 p.m. on Sunday. (606) 261-4212. It is located at the foot of the suspension bridge about 6 blocks east of I-75. Dress is informal, all beverages are served (including Sunday), and reservations are preferred. AE, CB, DC, MC, V. ($$$)

MIKE FINK HALIBUT NATCHEZ

2 ounces butter
½ ounce shallots
Pinch of freeze-dried
  chives
¼ to ½ ounce Chablis
6 ounces halibut

2 shrimp, shelled
2 ounces Alaskan king
  crabmeat
About ½ cup mushroom
  caps
Parsley flakes for garnish

Melt butter in skillet over medium heat, add shallots and chives. Pour in wine; bring to simmer. Add remaining ingredients. Increase temperature, allow to bubble until fish is firm. Serve at once, garnished with parsley flakes. Serves one.

MIKE FINK BANANAS FOSTER FLAMBÉ

1 Tablespoon butter
2 Tablespoons dark brown
  sugar
1 banana, quartered

½ ounce 80-proof white
  rum
Cinnamon
Vanilla ice cream

Melt butter in small saucepan over medium heat. Stir in sugar, increase temperature, and add banana. When bubbling, add rum and while flaming, sprinkle with cinnamon. Remove from heat; serve bananas over scoops of ice cream and top with remaining sauce. Serves two.

MIKE FINK SAUTÉED SEAFOOD SUPREME

½ pound butter
½ ounce shallots
Pinch of freeze-dried chives
¼ to ½ ounce Chablis
6 ounces Alaskan king crabmeat

6 shrimp, shelled
About ½ cup fresh mushroom caps
Large crouton or toast points
Parsley flakes for garnish

Melt butter in skillet over medium heat; add shallots and chives. Pour in wine, bring to simmer. Add remaining ingredients. When bubbling hot, lay seafood over crouton and spoon on remaining sauce. Sprinkle with parsley flakes and serve at once. Serves two.

THE MIKE FINK SANDWICH

2 slices white bread, toasted
6 ounces turkey breast, sliced
4 ounces cream sauce (see below)
1 Tablespoon fresh mushrooms sliced

Sharp Cheddar cheese, grated
3 slices bacon, cooked
Few sprinkles of paprika
Fresh parsley, chopped

Lay toast on heatproof platter and top with turkey. Stir mushrooms into cream sauce, spoon over turkey. Top with cheese; brown under broiler. Put bacon on top, sprinkle with paprika, and garnish with parsley. Serves one.

Cream sauce: blend 1 Tablespoon butter and 1 Tablespoon flour in saucepan over low heat. Add a generous ½ cup hot milk, and whisk until thickened and smooth. Season with salt and pepper.

DEE FELICE CAFÉ
Covington

DURING THE PERIOD OF

western expansion, many immigrants headed down the Ohio River, and a number of them settled in the bustling little city of Covington. Chiefly of German origin, newcomers brought skills with them—there were artisans of all types, merchants, industrialists, and professionals.

In 1868, James G. Arnold, a prominent Covington builder, contracted to erect three 3-story commercial buildings. The brick structure at the northwest corner of Main and 6th Streets was to house three businesses on the street level, and "a commodious hall for public meetings" above.

Edward L. Pieck, a Covington native of German extraction and a graduate pharmacist, moved into the corner store in 1885. Other tenants were a confectioner and a barber downstairs, and the I.O.O.F. (Odd Fellows) Hall on the 3rd floor.

By 1890, Pieck had expanded into the center store, opening the wall between and supporting the span with slender columns. Pictures at that time show hand-carved cherry cabinets, a molded tin ceiling, and a marble floor, with a cast iron storefront; few changes have been made, although two elegant rooms, with stained glass windows, a tented ceiling, and magnificent oak mantels, were added at the rear around the turn of the century.

The building remained a pharmacy until 1971, when it became an antiques shop. As part of the West Side/Main Strasse Historic District, it was placed on the National Register.

Dee Felice, a popular Cincinnati jazz musician and band leader who has traveled and performed with Mel Torme, Julius La Rosa, James Brown, and Sergio Mendez, had searched for a place in which to open a jazz club and restaurant. The corner store was perfect, and the café opened in March of 1984, its Victorian refinements virtually unspoiled.

The embossed tin ceiling was picked out in gold leaf, and the wide molded tin cornice and frieze were enhanced with paint in gray and unusual shades of pink. Back rooms are now intimate dining rooms, and the third store has been included, with arches into the main room where Felice holds forth on a stage behind the bar, playing jazz with his big

(12 piece) band on Mondays and his Sleepcat Dixieland Band on weekends.

Guests enjoy the blend of foods on the menu; Chef Gene Alderson offers fiery New Orleans entrées (just right with jazz) homemade pastas, steaks, and chef's specialties such as Chicken Martinelli (boneless breast, braised with oysters, herb butter, and sparkling apple cider), veal and seafood. Desserts include a fine chocolate mousse, chocolate pecan pie, and an unusual cheesecake that is half strawberry and half chocolate.

Dee Felice Café, 529 Main Street, Covington, Kentucky 41011, is open from 3 p.m. to 2:30 a.m., 7 days a week. The "Raw Bar" of seafood is open 3 to 5 p.m., every day but Saturday. Dinner is served 5 p.m. to 11 p.m. Monday through Thursday; to 12 p.m. Friday and Saturday; and to 10 p.m. on Sunday. (606)261-2365. There is jazz every night but Tuesday, with a jam session from 4 to 7 p.m. on Sunday. Dress is casual, and all beverages are served, including Sunday; reservations are requested, especially on weekends. AE, DC, MC, V. ($$)

DEE FELICE CAFÉ MUSSELS GINO

1 ounce butter
A "tad" of garlic
A "tad" of shallots
14 mussels, in the shell
3 Tablespoons chopped
   parsley
Salt and pepper to taste
⅔ cup good white dry wine
Lemon wedge for garnish

In saucepan, heat butter with garlic and shallots until hot. Add mussels, parsley, salt and pepper. Sprinkle with wine, cover, and steam until done, about four or five minutes. Serve opened mussels in a ring with a lemon wedge. Serves one.

DEE FELICE CAFÉ STUFFED SOLE

Two 4 to 6-ounce lemon
   sole filets
1 medium tomato, chopped
1 medium onion, chopped
¼ pound crawfish
¼ pound crabmeat
¼ pound shrimp
Pinch of chervil
Salt and pepper to taste
Paprika
Hollandaise or Bernaise
   sauce

40

On oiled tray, place one filet of sole; top with vegetables and seafood, and season to taste with chervil, salt and pepper. Place second filet on top, sprinkle with paprika, and bake at 350 degrees for eight minutes. Top with Hollandaise or Bernaise sauce. Serves one.

DEE FELICE CAFÉ CHICKEN MARTINELLI

1 chicken breast, split and boned
Olive oil for sautéeing
Brandy and white wine
5 oysters, floured and deep fried
3 ounces chicken stock

3 ounces sparkling apple cider
4 ounces butter, cut in cubes
Pinch of basil
Salt and pepper to taste

Sauté chicken in oil; deglaze pan with brandy and white wine. Add oysters, chicken stock and apple cider, then butter cubes. When thickened, season with basil, salt, and pepper. Serves one.

DEE FELICE CAFÉ NEW ORLEANS CLAM CHOWDER

½ pound butter
2 onions, chopped
½ bunch celery, chopped
1 ½ carrots, chopped
2 zucchini, chopped
2 yellow squash, chopped
Pinch of nutmeg
¼ teaspoon thyme
¼ teaspoon cayenne
3 or 4 bay leaves
Salt and pepper

1 cup flour
1 cup yellow cornmeal
1 ½ gallons clam juice or seafood stock
½ gallon fish stock
1 gallon clams, quartered
1 ½ quarts heavy cream
1 ½ cups sauterne
1 ½ pound okra, cut into rings

In saucepan, melt butter and sauté vegetables five to ten minutes. Place vegetables in large pot, add spices, then slowly add flour, cornmeal, clam juice or seafood stock, and fish stock. Bring to boil for ten minutes and add clams. Simmer for five minutes and add cream and white wine. Three minutes before serving, add okra, taste, and reseason. Serves 20.

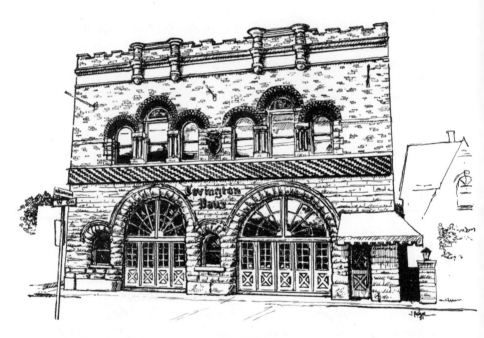

MICK NOLL'S COVINGTON HAUS
Covington

WHEN COVINGTON FIRE

station No. 1 was completed in 1898, it was described in a local newspaper as "modern in every requirement, with sleeping apartments for 25 firemen . . . supplemented with every convenience, including baths and gymnasium."

Many of Fire Chief Meyers' ideas were used in the design by local architect Daniel Seger, which may have incorporated part of a pre-1877 building. What made the building unusual was its construction: the second floor is suspended from a steel truss on the roof, leaving a clear span on the first floor to house fire wagons and other machinery without obstruction.

Wheels fitted into grooves in the floor, so that engines were always parked in the same location; harnesses, suspended from the ceiling, dropped down onto waiting horses and were swiftly buckled into place. As the huge doors swung open, the entire equipage, complete with firemen in boots and slickers, sped to the fire minutes after the alarm sounded.

After horse-drawn equipment was replaced by gasoline powered fire trucks, the engine house continued in its original use until a new fire station was built elsewhere in 1975. "The fire engines moved out when we moved in," owner Mick Noll said. The building was placed on the National Register in 1983 as part of Covington's Downtown Commercial Historic District.

Because the public would be using the second floor, huge posts, each cut from the heart of a fir tree, were brought in from Portland, Oregon for additional support. The former stable was converted to a bar, with ladders, boots, slickers, firemen's hats, and other relics of the fire station era used as decoration. Stained glass mosaics now fill the arched doorways, and crowds of merrymakers dine where steam engines used to stand.

"We tried to save as much (of the building) as we could," said Noll, who describes the food at his Covington Haus as "German-Irish, using native foods and spices and local products to make basic meat and potatoes exciting for everybody."

A festival nearly every month contributes to the fun: St. Patrick's Day and Oktoberfest are enormously popular, with a wine festival in November, Garlicfest in January, German Fasching in February, and a German band every Saturday night for dancing. The roof garden, open in summer, overlooks the Cincinnati skyline and the Mutter Gottes church across the street.

The Hot Daily Buffet saves time at lunch; there's also Sausage Kabob with sauerkraut and potato pancake, salads, soups and sandwiches, and such German dishes as Sauerbraten and Spaetzle (beef and noodles), and Jaegerschnitzel (pork cutlet in mushroom sauce), plus steaks and seafoods. Dinner offers larger portions of the same, with additional appetizer, chicken, seafood, and steak choices. Homemade desserts include pies, cheesecake, and traditional German Black Forest Cake.

Mick Noll's Covington Haus, 100 West 6th Street, Covington, Kentucky 41011, is open from 11 a.m. to 1 a.m., with continous service until 10 p.m. on Friday and Saturday, until 9 p.m. on Sunday. Snacks are available after the kitchen closes. (606)261-6655. Dress is casual and all beverages are served, including Sunday; reservations are requested and advisable on weekends. AE, DC, MC, V. ($$)

MICK NOLL'S SAUERKRAUT BALLS

1 medium onion, minced
½ rib celery, minced
1 Tablespoon butter
3 pounds Boston butt, ground
2 stale hard rolls, grated

1 pound sauerkraut, well drained and ground
2 eggs, lightly beaten
1 egg, beaten, for egg wash
Milk, for egg wash
Cracker meal for breading

In large skillet, sauté onion and celery in butter; do not brown. Add pork and cook just until done, then set aside.

In large mixing bowl, mix pork mixture with grated roll crumbs, sauerkraut, and eggs, and blend to a smooth consistency, adding more egg or crumbs if necessary. Shape mixture into balls about ¾" in diameter, chill, dip in egg wash made of one egg beaten with a little milk, and roll in cracker meal. Deep fry at 350 degrees until brown, and serve at once. Mick Noll suggests this amount for "a big party."

MICK NOLL'S POTATO PANCAKES

8 medium potatoes
1 large onion
2 eggs, beaten
2 Tablespoons flour

2 Tablespoons minced
   parsley
Salt and pepper

In saucepan, boil potatoes until just done. Refrigerate.

Peel and grate cold potatoes and onions. Mix with eggs, flour, parsley, salt and pepper. Form mixture with hands into cakes ½" to ¾" thick, about 3 ½" to 4" in diameter. Fry in deep fat or pan fry just long enough to brown. Serves six.

MICK NOLL'S BLACK FOREST CAKE

2 cups pitted dark sweet
   cherries, with juice
Kirsch liqueur
One 1-inch layer yellow
   cake
Two 1-inch layers
   chocolate cake

1 teaspoon plain gelatin
2 cups whipping cream
Powdered sugar to taste
3 ounces semi-sweet
   chocolate, grated
Red cherries with stems,
   optional

In saucepan, cook down cherries until thickened; cool, and add kirsch as desired.

Sprinkle cake layers with kirsch. Dissolve gelatin in small amount of kirsch, and set aside.

In mixing bowl, whip cream adding sugar to taste, dissolved gelatin, and more kirsch as cream thickens.

Spread scant ¼ of whipped cream on one chocolate layer. Top with half of cherries, pressing cherries down into cream. Place yellow layer on top, add another ¼ of cream, then press rest of cherries into cream. Place last chocolate layer on top, and cover sides and top of cake with rest of cream. Sprinkle grated chocolate on top. Red cherries with stems may be used as a garnish.

deSHĀ'S
Lexington

$\mathbf{I}$N JUNE, 1775, A BAND OF frontiersmen camped at a wilderness spring in the "Great Meadow." A pleasant spot, with ample water and good hunting, it seemed an ideal location for a settlement. As the men, including Robert Patterson and Simon Kenton, were discussing the recent news of the first battle of the Revolution, they named the prospective town for that battle, at Lexington, Massachusetts.

It was four years before Patterson was able to return to Lexington; with 25 men from Harrodsburg, he built a blockhouse near the middle fork of Elkhorn Creek in April of 1779. The blockhouse became one corner of a fort encircling an "unfailing" spring, lying between today's Mill Street and Broadway, south of Main Street.

A town was laid out, and a log courthouse was constructed at the corner of Broadway (then called "Main Crossing') and Main Street. When the courthouse was relocated to its present site, the earlier building was used as the printing office of the "Kentucky Gazette," which was published from 1787 to 1848.

During the 1870's and 80's, a period of great prosperity in Lexington, a group of commercial buildings were constructed in the block bounded by Broadway, Main, Short, and Spring Streets. These handsome buildings, incorporating such Victorian embellishments as bracketed storefronts, ornate hood moldings, and pressed tin ceilings, housed a variety of firms. Lower floors were used as retail and manufacturing space, and owners often lived above. The Victorian Commercial Block was listed on the National Register in 1978, and was adapted for use as a shopping mall in 1985.

The three-story brick structure on the corner of Main and Broadway is attributed to Phelix Lundin, a Swedish architect who is believed to have designed nine buildings on Main Street during the 1870's. The building was always divided into two business houses, but has now become one—brand new deShā's restaurant. Although the interior has been greatly altered, an effort has been made to preserve the Victorian feeling, incorporating reproduction lighting fixtures and tin ceilings, oak paneling and trim, and a bar from one of Lexington's historic hostelries.

At deShā's, guests may have a snack, an appetizer, or a complete meal, chosen from a list that includes homemade chili or soup with sour-cream cornbread, sandwiches and burgers, daily special entrées (often fresh seafood), homemade fruit cobbler and Chocolate Fudge Brownie Fix. Food quality is stressed, and owner Nick Sanders describes deShā's as a "fun or casual place, with a lively atmosphere and upbeat music in the background."

deShā's, 101 North Broadway, Lexington, Kentucky 40507, is open from 11 a.m. until "late night," with continuous service, Monday through Saturday and possibly Sunday. (606)259-3771. Dress is casual, all beverages are served, and reservations are accepted for groups of eight or more. AE, DC, MC, V. ($)

deSHĀ'S CORNBREAD

2 cups self-rising cornmeal   3 cups sour cream
6 eggs   1 ½ cups salad oil
20 ounces cream style corn   ⅓ cup sugar

Combine all ingredients, mixing well. Pour into well-greased 15" x 10" x 2" pan. Bake at 350 degrees for about 40 minutes, or until a pick comes out clean.

deSHĀ'S CHILI

1 cup chopped onions   2 Tablespoons chili powder
2 ½ pounds ground chuck   1 teaspoon garlic powder
2 pounds kidney beans   12 ounces tomato juice
3 pounds tomatoes,   1 Tablespoon salt
  chopped
2 Tablespoons brown
  sugar

In large skillet, brown onions and ground chuck, stirring, until done. Mix in all other ingredients, and cook over medium high heat about 15 minutes, then simmer for one hour or until relatively thick.

de SHĀ'S HAWAIIAN CHICKEN SALAD

1 pound cooked white meat
  of chicken, cut bite-sized
½ cup mayonnaise
1 green onion, chopped

1 cup canned chunky
  pineapple, drained
1 cup chopped pecans

In mixing bowl, combine chicken, mayonnaise, and green onion and mix well. Stir in pineapple and nuts.

deSHĀ'S CRAN-APPLE COBBLER

3 cups sliced apples
2 cups chopped fresh
  cranberries
¾ cup light corn syrup
1 cup flour

¾ cup sugar
1 ½ teaspoons cinnamon
½ cup mayonnaise
½ cup chopped pecans

Grease 9" x 13" x 2" pan. In a mixing bowl, toss together apples, cranberries, and syrup. Spread mixture evenly over bottom of pan.

In a mixing bowl, stir together flour, sugar, and cinnamon. With pastry blender, cut in mayonnaise until mixture resembles coarse crumbs. Stir in nuts and sprinkle over fruit. Bake at 350 degrees for 30 to 35 minutes or until lightly browned.

DUDLEY'S RESTAURANT
Lexington

LEXINGTON CITY SCHOOL

No. 3, known as The Dudley School, was constructed in 1881 on the site of an earlier residence which had housed the school since its creation in 1851. It was named for Dr. Benjamin Winslow Dudley, a prominent Lexington surgeon and chairman of anatomy and surgery departments at Transylvania University Medical School.

The two-story, late Richardsonian brick structure continued as a school until 1932. Among early instructors was Mary Desha, one of four founders of the Daughters of the American Revolution.

The building, an important landmark in South Hill Historic District, had housed various government offices during depression and war years, but stood vacant for seven years before restoration. With the South Hill Historic District, it was placed on the National Register in 1978, and in 1980 it became Dudley Square, a unique mall of specialty shops and Dudley's Restaurant.

Owners Deborah Long and John Shea carefully adapted available space for their restaurant; permission was given by The Bluegrass Trust for a glass-enclosed hallway between the former principal's office and a classroom, and kitchens in "catacombs" in the basement were vented four floors to the roof. An enormous oak back bar, from a restaurant closed by prohibition, required an entire day and ten people to move; five people were needed to lift the mirror.

Today, entered from the wide hallway that echoes with the footsteps of generations of schoolchildren, Dudley's seems always to have existed as a restaurant. The restful colors of plum and green are set off by natural wood and plants; the bar is cozy and intimate, and the dining room, lighted by tall windows, is graced with linens, candles, and flowers. It serves as a gallery for local artists. In warm weather, diners linger on the patio under umbrellas and a large sycamore tree to listen to the fountain.

Food at Dudley's receives extra attention: everything is fresh and cooked to order, accommodating those on special diets. Local foods are treated in non-traditional ways, with daily appetizer, soup, fish and seafood specials, and a menu of "regulars." Appetizers and pastas are especially creative, as are rich, sweet desserts, and all entrées are served with salad or soup of the day. Hot muffins are different each day, often combining many flavoring ingredients, and are always superb.

Dudley's Restaurant, 380 S. Mill St., Lexington, Kentucky 40508, is open for lunch from 11:30 a.m. to 2:30 p.m., Monday through Saturday, and for dinner from 5:30 to 10 p.m. Monday through Thursday, until 11 p.m. Friday and Saturday. Lighter fare is available from 2:30 to 5:30 in the bar. (606)252-1010. Dress is casual, all beverages are served, and reservations are always a good idea, and are essential on weekends. AE, MC, V. ($$)

DUDLEY'S POPPYSEED MUFFINS

2 cups flour	1 ¼ cups milk
¼ cup sugar	1 egg
Pinch of salt	¼ cup dark corn syrup
2 heaping teaspoons baking powder	¼ cup melted butter
	2 Tablespoons poppyseed

Mix all ingredients in order, being careful not to overmix. Spoon into greased muffin tins, and bake at 350 degrees for 15 to 20 minutes in regular oven, about 12 minutes in convection oven. To vary flavor, substitute ¼ cup raisins, nuts, or drained crushed pineapple for the poppyseed, or use 1 teaspoon cinnamon, ginger, or other spice, or a combination. Brown sugar may be substituted for granulated, or honey for corn syrup. Possibilities are unlimited! Yields one dozen large muffins.

DUDLEY'S LEMON VEAL

1 cup veal or chicken stock	Salt and pepper
1 cup white wine	1 to 1 ½ pounds veal top round, sliced as thin as possible
2 Tablespoons butter	
2 Tablespoons flour	
1 cup heavy cream, heated	Flour for dredging
Juice of 2 lemons	Butter for sautéeing
¼ cup chopped parsley	

Mix stock and white wine and reduce to 1 cup. Blend butter and flour in saucepan over low heat; use some of this mixture to thicken stock/wine mixture to heavy cream consistancy— all may not be required. Add cream, then lemon juice and parsley. Season to taste and keep warm. Pound veal thin; dredge in flour and sauté in butter until done. Remove veal and pour off excess butter. Deglaze pan with lemon sauce and pour over veal. Serves four.

DUDLEY'S CHOCOLATE CHEESE PIE

One 9-inch deep-dish
  graham cracker or
  regular pie shell, baked
8 ounces cream cheese,
  softened
¾ cup brown sugar
Pinch of salt

1 teaspoon vanilla
2 large eggs, separated
6 ounces semi-sweet choc-
  olate, melted
1 cup heavy cream,
  whipped

In large mixing bowl, combine cream cheese, sugar, salt, vanilla, and yolks, and beat until well blended. Beat in melted chocolate. In another bowl, beat egg whites until stiff; fold, with whipped cream, into chocolate-cheese mixture. When blended, pour into prepared pie shell and chill. Serves eight.

CASA EXECUTIVA
(EXECUTIVE HOUSE)
Lexington

IN 1781, THE VIRGINIA General Assembly was petitioned by Lexington's Board of Trustees (Kentucky did not become a separate state until 1792) to allow the addition of 710 acres of land just south of the existing town.

Beginning at the Town Branch, or Middle Fork of The Elkhorn, which ran approximately where Vine Street does now, the new portion of Lexington was on an elevation which had long been called the "South Hill."

South Hill represents 19th-century development of Lexington; Federal and Greek Revival townhouses rub elbows with cottages and impressive houses of the Victorian period, and later construction of churches, a school, and commercial buildings resulted in an interesting architectural mix. The South Hill Historic District was placed on the National Register in 1978.

The house at 270 S. Limestone (often called "Lime" by natives) was designed about 1880 by John McMurtry, a well-known Lexington architect and builder, for Judge J. Soule Smith. It was evidently built in two different stages, the addition to the north more than doubling the original space.

Judge Smith, a lawyer, at one time county attorney, and correspondent known as "Falcon" for the *Louisville Times,* was also author of "The Mint Julep," in which instructions for preparing that Kentucky delicacy were set down. It seems fitting that in 1978 his house became a restaurant, where fine foods and beverages are served once again.

When Chef Giovanni Freda and his wife/manager Mae bought the house in 1975, it was scheduled to be demolished, but Chef Freda remembered the house from visits while he was in college, and determined to save it. A fine staircase, handmade poplar moldings, and eight fireplaces were restored with the same care used in their creation; a sprinkler system and heating and air conditioning were added, and all plumbing and wiring replaced, but the spirit of the house is still that of the 1880's.

Continental cuisine is presented at award-winning Casa Executiva, with complete French tableside service. Chef Freda, who says "people eat with their senses," is particular about freshness and presentation, and has popularized locally such items as mussels, monkfish, and shark.

All breads, pastries, and desserts are made on the premises, and all meats are hand cut. Veal is a specialty here, with at least ten veal items on a menu that also includes numerous appetizers, soups, fresh seafoods, steaks, pastas, and such classic desserts as Baked Alaska and Cherries Jubilee. Guests should remember Chef Freda's invitation: "What we have on the menu is just the beginning."

Casa Executiva (Executive House), 270 S. Limestone Street, Lexington, Kentucky 40508, is open for dinner only, 5 to 11 p.m., Monday through Saturday. Parties of 20 or more may be scheduled at other times by prior arrangement. (606)254-6263. Dress is casual, excepting shorts, tennis shoes, etc., but jackets for men are preferred. All beverages are served, including an extensive wine list; reservations are preferred, especially weekends and during football and racing seasons (April and October-December). Half portions are available for children. AE, CB, D, MC, V. ($$$)

CASA EXECUTIVA VEAL PATRIZZIA

6 Tablespoons butter, divided	1 Tablespoon grated Parmesan cheese
8 medium mushrooms, sliced	4 veal cutlets, 8-10 ounces each
Salt and pepper	½ cup Chablis
8 Tablespoons heavy cream	2 Tablespoons chopped parsley

In a small skillet, melt 2 tablespoons butter over moderately high heat. Add mushrooms, season with salt and pepper, and sauté until softened. Stir in cream and Parmesan cheese until sauce is thickened; set aside.

In a larger skillet, melt 4 tablespoons butter, add veal and sprinkle on salt and pepper. Cook 6 to 7 minutes, remove from skillet, and set aside on warm platter.

Add Chablis to skillet, stirring over high heat to deglaze skillet; pour mushroom/cream mixture into Chablis, and heat to boiling. Pour sauce over veal and sprinkle with fresh parsley. Serves four.

CASA EXECUTIVA BISTECCA ALLA PIZZAIOLA

Four 10-ounce New York
  Strips
Olive oil for sautéeing
2 cloves garlic, crushed
¾ cup diced onion
3 sprigs oregano

3 sprigs basil
Salt and pepper to taste
1 ½ cups peeled, diced
  tomatoes
Fresh chopped parsley

Pound beef very thin. In large sauté pan, heat olive oil; brown meat, then add garlic, onion, spices and seasonings. Sauté 4 minutes, add tomatoes and cook 5 more minutes. Serve beef slices smothered with tomato sauce and sprinkled with parsley. Serves four.

MOZZARELLA ITALIA

3 eggs, beaten
½ Tablespoon Parmesan
  Cheese, grated
Salt and pepper to taste
Fresh chopped parsley

24 ounces whole milk
  mozzarella cheese, in 12
  slices
Flour for dredging
Olive oil for sautéeing

In mixing bowl, beat eggs with cheese, salt, pepper, and parsley. Dust mozzarella lightly with flour and drop into eggs.

In large sauté pan, heat oil and sauté cheese slices until golden brown. Remove to paper towels to drain. Serve coated with marinara sauce; serves six.

For marinara sauce:
½ cup diced onions
Olive oil for sautéeing
1 clove garlic, crushed
Pinch each basil and
  oregano

Salt and pepper to taste
1 cup peeled, diced
  tomatoes

In a sauté pan, sauté onions in oil until soft; add garlic, spices, and seasonings, and sauté 3 minutes. Add tomatoes and cook about 5 more minutes.

MERRICK INN
Lexington

IN THE BLUEGRASS RE-
gion, famed for the excellence of its horses, none has received
the acclaim of Merrick, who finished "in the money" 157 times
of 203 starts. He won 64 of those races, and continued to
race to a great age, running 3 times in his 12-year-old season.
When he died at the age of 38 in 1941, he was the oldest of
all recorded thoroughbreds.

His name lived on in the famous horse farm of J. Cal Milam,
owner and trainer of other famous horses: Exterminator,
Derby winner of 1918, Anna M. Humphrey, Tut Tut, Commodore, Brown Wisdom, Milkmaid, McKee, and Dust Flower.

The rolling green fields where they grazed have been sub-
merged in suburban growth, and an apartment complex is
now entered through the farm's grey stone gates, but the
manor house is still known for its style and fine food.

Bordered by trim Colonial-style townhouses, the tree-lined
entrance is named for Mr. Milam. Guests are cautioned to
"look for a house with no signs and lots of cars"—the residential atmosphere is rigidly maintained.

Encircled by shrubbery, Merrick Inn's welcoming porch
signals the warmth within. An 18th century atmosphere pre-
vails, with comfortable reproduction furniture, carefully chosen wallpapers, and handsome prints on the walls. Operated
as a restaurant by Bob and Libby Murray since the early
1970's, Merrick Inn's popularity stems from food that represents the best of Regional American Cooking.

"There's no better food available than we grow right here
in this country," Bob Murray said. "If it's well prepared, you
can't beat it."

Following this philosophy, food at Merrick Place is fresh
and simply prepared, without heavy sauces that might obscure the natural flavors. Prime rib, steaks, lamb chops, country ham, and chicken are always available, and a host of
choices such as trout (stuffed with cornbread, crab and
shrimp), wall-eye pike, chicken breasts sautéed with Bing
cherries, and roast pork loin (with applesauce and dressing)
reflect availability.

Served at fireside on brisk winter nights, Merrick Place
food has a comforting quality, but lighter summer fare and

salads are equally notable. The limestone Bibb lettuce salad with cucumber dressing is especially popular; vegetables are fresh and often ingeniously prepared, and hot rolls and muffins and desserts, all homemade, add the final touch to a memorable meal.

Merrick Inn, 3333 Wood Valley Court, Lexington, Kentucky 40502, is open for dinner only, Monday through Thursday from 5:30 to 10 p.m., until 10:30 Friday and Saturday. It is closed the first week in January. (606)269-5417. Merrick Place is just inside the New Circle Road (Circle 4), east of Tate's Creek Pike, across from The Lansdowne Shoppes; follow Milam Lane to Merrick Inn. Dress is "casual in good taste," all beverages are served, and reservations are almost a necessity. AE, MC, V. ($$)

MERRICK INN CUCUMBER DRESSING

2 large cucumbers, peeled, seeded, and chopped fine
2 cups mayonnaise
⅔ cup sour cream
2 medium green onions, chopped
2 teaspoons sugar
Salt and pepper

Allow cucumbers to drain thoroughly, or the dressing will be watery. In a bowl, mix mayonnaise, sour cream, onions, and sugar; add drained cucumber with salt and pepper to taste. This dressing is excellent with home grown tomatoes or spring lettuce. Yields about 3 cups.

MERRICK INN SQUASH CASSEROLE

5-6 small squash, yellow or a mixture of yellow and zucchini
1 cup medium sharp Cheddar cheese, diced
3 Tablespoons pimientos, chopped
3 Tablespoons onion, chopped
1 cup cracker crumbs
3 Tablespoons melted butter
2 large eggs, well beaten
Salt and pepper
1 cup milk, scalded

Slice squash, cook until tender, and mash to make 2 cups. In a bowl, combine squash with all ingredients except milk;

mix well. Scald milk and cool slightly; stir into squash mixture. Pour into buttered 1 ½ quart casserole dish and bake one hour at 350 degrees. Serves six or eight.

MERRICK INN CRAB CAKES

1 pound fresh backfin crab meat	½ cup mayonnaise
2 hard cooked eggs, finely grated	1 teaspoon prepared mustard
1 Tablespoon finely chopped parsley	1 teaspoon salt
	White pepper to taste
	6 soda crackers, crushed

Clean crab, removing all cartilage and bone. In bowl, mix remaining ingredients, except crackers; add crab meat. Mix lightly and refrigerate. Form mixture into eight cakes and roll in crushed crackers. Deep fry at 340 degrees or sauté until golden. Serve plain with lemon or with a sauce. Serves four.

MERRICK INN GERMAN SWEET CHOCOLATE PIE

One 8-inch unbaked pie shell	1 ½ cups granulated sugar
4 ounces German sweet chocolate	3 teaspoons cornstarch
¼ cup butter	⅛ teaspoon salt
One 13-ounce can evaporated milk	2 eggs, slightly beaten
	1 teaspoon vanilla
	1 ⅓ cups shredded coconut
	½ cup chopped pecans

Melt chocolate with butter over low heat. Stir until blended; remove from heat, and stir in milk. In bowl, combine sugar, cornstarch, and salt; beat in eggs and vanilla, then chocolate mixture. Pour into pie shell. Combine coconut and nuts and sprinkle over pie; bake at 375 degrees for 45 to 50 minutes. Cool for 4 hours. Serves six.

Note: Wrap aluminum foil around edge of pie to prevent over-browning; remove after 25 minutes of baking.

THE MANSION AT GRIFFIN GATE
Lexington

WHEN DANIEL BOONE
and other early explorers of Kentucky returned to "The
Settlements," they enthusiastically described the Bluegrass region as "The Eden of the West." Rich in trees, water,
and game, the lush center of Kentucky attracted thousands.

The gentleman farmer tradition, brought from Virginia
by many of her younger sons, is epitomized by comfortable
country homes, a leisured way of life, and the graciousness
that has come to be known as "Kentucky hospitality."

Evidence of this may still be seen by the visitor who drives
out the old roads that radiate from Lexington like spokes
from a hub. Secluded in clumps of trees, handsome houses
preside over fields of magnificent horses, surrounded by miles
of stone or painted board fences.

The Newtown Pike, north of town, passes industrial development and University of Kentucky farms, to enter rolling
green countryside. Near the I-64 interchange, centering a golf
course and a cluster of motel development, is a lovely old
house now called "The Mansion at Griffin Gate."

The house, designated a Kentucky Landmark, was originally designed by Cincinnatus Shryock, a respected Kentucky
architect, and was built in 1873 on the site of an earlier house.
A two-story red brick with a cupola and a one-story porch,
it was called "Highland Home," and was the boyhood home
of Kentucky historian J. Winston Coleman. After the house
was sold in the 1920's, the cupola and porch were removed,
and the pedimented 2-story porch with Ionic columns was
added.

Subsequent owners changed the name to "Griffin Gate"
for the winged figures on the entrance gates, brought in antique mantels and lighting fixtures, and attached several one-
story additions. Although details of the 1873 structure are
barely recognizable, the resulting house is most attractive.

Today it is a fine restaurant, part of Marriott's Griffin Gate
Resort, presenting Regional American Cuisine in eight comfortable dining rooms and on the patio in warm weather.
Menus change seasonally and with the availability of fresh
ingredients; such favorites as the Williamsburg Sauté (veal
and shrimp), steaks, broiled seafoods, and barbecue shrimp
are, however, usually available.

For lunch, Chef Art Howard offers lighter entrées, sandwiches, and clever salads, plus a daily Mansion Special "with a Kentucky Flavor." At any meal, hot breads, appetizers such as Scallops and Artichoke Hearts sautéed in Brandy, and rich desserts—try the Chocolate Macadamia Nut Cream Cheese Pie, or Kentucky Bourbon Bread Pudding with Warm Bourbon Sauce—make dining at The Mansion at Griffin Gate unforgettable.

The Mansion at Griffin Gate, 1720 Newtown Pike, Lexington, Kentucky 40511, is open for lunch Monday through Friday, 11 a.m. to 2 p.m., and for dinner 6 to 10 p.m. Monday through Thursday, 6 to 10:30 p.m. Friday and Saturday, and 5 to 9 p.m. on Sunday. (606)231-5152. Coat and tie are preferred for men, but dress code is relaxed in summer; all beverages are available, and reservations are almost a necessity. AE, CB, D, MC, V. ($$$)

THE MANSION PIKE WITH WALNUT BUTTER

Eight 8-ounce filets of pike   **8 ounces CLARIFIED**
Salt and pepper   **butter OR vegetable oil**
Flour for dredging   **Walnut butter (see below)**

Skin pike filets, season with salt and pepper, and dredge lightly in flour. Sauté in hot CLARIFIED butter or vegetable oil until done. Remove to plates and top each filet with one tablespoon of walnut butter. Allow butter to melt over the filets before serving. Serves eight.

For walnut butter:
1 cup walnuts, toasted   **1 Tablespoon lemon juice**
1 pound lightly salted   **¼ cup Frangelica liqueur**
butter, softened

Combine all ingredients and blend well.

THE MANSION PEPPERCORN STRIP STEAK WITH GARLIC-MUSTARD BUTTER

Four 12-ounce New York   **4 Tablespoons peanut oil**
Strips   **Garlic-mustard butter (see**
Black peppercorns,   **below)**
cracked

Coat steaks well with peppercorns and pan-fry in hot oil, turning once. Remove to plate and glaze hot steaks with garlic-mustard butter. Serves four.

For garlic-mustard butter:

½ **pound butter, softened**	¼ **cup Creole mustard**
2 cloves garlic, minced	**1 teaspoon tarragon**

Combine ingredients and mix until smooth. Hold at room temperature.

THE MANSION ALMOND CHOCOLATE MOUSSE

2 cups whipping cream	½ **cup powdered sugar**
3 ounces butter	¼ **cup hot coffee**
1 pound Tobler semi-sweet	¼ **cup Amaretto liqueur**
chocolate	**Sliced almonds, toasted**
3 eggs, divided	

Whip cream until stiff; chill. In a double boiler over hot water, melt butter with chocolate. In a small bowl, beat egg yolks with sugar until thick and lemon colored.

Add hot coffee to melted chocolate, beat yolk/sugar mixture and Amaretto into mixture and chill to slightly below room temperature.

Beat egg whites until stiff. Fold whipped cream into chocolate, then fold in beaten egg whites. Chill at least two hours before serving. Garnish with almonds. Serves eight.

ACADEMY INN
Lancaster

PIONEERS WERE ALWAYS
on the move, and trails in the wilderness were important
connections between outposts. The road from Boonesboro,
Daniel Boone's first fort, to Harrodsburg, the first permanent
settlement in Kentucky, was heavily traveled. Where it inter-
sected with the Lexington-Crab Orchard route, a band of
Pennsylvanians established a little crossroads community in
1798. They called it "Lancaster," for their former home in
Pennsylvania.

That same year, the Kentucky Legislature granted a char-
ter to The Lancaster Male Academy, which has been located
at the corner of Campbell and Buford Streets since 1806. At
least one early schoolhouse burned, but evidence of schoolboy
occupation may still be seen in the 1875 Victorian cottage
which remains. Boys with knives must leave their marks—
and often their names— for posterity.

Students would have enjoyed the home-like atmosphere
that characterizes The Academy Inn today. Painted a cheerful
yellow, the deceptively small brick building wears a residential air, and sits in a quiet lawn just a block from US 27.
With other lots from the original town plan, it is on the National Register of Historic Places. Academy Inn is not far
from the birthplace of militant prohibitionist Carry A. Nation.

Three dining rooms and a large hall in which guests may
be seated are decorated in Colonial style, with soft sage green
and cream the predominant colors. In two cozy parlor-like
rooms, dark round tables seating four cluster around fireplaces; larger tables in the big room are gauged to family
groups or local organizations.

Opened in 1983 by Michael and Donna Botkin, The Academy Inn fulfills a real need in Lancaster. Parties, meetings,
and wedding receptions are frequent, but out-of-town visitors
are equally welcome. Lunch and dinner menus are the same—
and the same reasonable cost—with the emphasis on what
Michael Botkin calls "real" products. "Everything we can
do ourselves, we do," he said. "It's as close as we can come
to home cooking."

Each day a different special joins country ham, chicken
salad and other Kentucky-flavored entrées; The Academy's

famous roast beef appears both as a main course and as a sandwich. Dainty "tea room" salads contrast with hearty sandwiches, and homemade soups, hot breads, and spectacular pies ensure a choice to please everyone.

The Academy Inn, 108 S. Campbell Street, Lancaster, Kentucky 40444, is open from 11 a.m. to 8 p.m. Tuesday through Saturday, with continuous service, and from 11 a.m. to 3 p.m. Sunday. (606)792-6237. Lancaster is about 30 miles south of Lexington via US 27. Dress is casual, and reservations are suggested for Sundays; no charge cards are accepted. ($)

ACADEMY INN MANDARIN ORANGE SALAD

One 3-ounce package
  lemon gelatin
One 3-ounce package
  orange gelatin
One 6-ounce can frozen
  orange juice
  concentrate, undiluted

Two 11-ounce cans
  mandarin oranges; juice
  from one can
One 15 ¼-ounce can
  crushed pineapple, with
  juice

In saucepan, dissolve gelatin in 2 cups boiling water. Add orange juice concentrate and juice from one can mandarin oranges. Refrigerate until slightly thickened, about 45 minutes. Add pineapple with juice and mandarin oranges. Pour into 9" x 13" pan or mold and chill until firm. Serves 16.

ACADEMY INN CHOCOLATE CREAM PIE

One 9-inch baked pie shell
2 cups milk
⅛ teaspoon salt
1 cup sugar
4 Tablespoons cornstarch

3 Tablespoons cocoa
2 egg yolks, beaten
3 Tablespoons butter
¼ teaspoon vanilla
Meringue (see below)

In double boiler over simmering water, scald milk. Combine salt, sugar, cornstarch, and cocoa; and stir into milk. Add a small amount of mixture to yolks to warm them, then stir egg mixture into hot milk. Continuing to stir, cook until thickened. Remove from heat and add butter and vanilla. Pour into pie shell, cool briefly, cover with meringue and bake at

350 degrees until meringue is light brown. Serves eight.

Meringue:

4 egg whites   6 Tablespoons sugar
½ teaspoon cream of tartar

Beat egg whites and cream of tartar; add sugar gradually and continue to beat until sugar is dissolved and egg whites are stiff but not dry. Mound on pie, sealing edges to pastry.

ACADEMY INN THOUSAND ISLAND SALAD DRESSING

1 ½ cups mayonnaise
1 medium onion, finely
  chopped
1 cup Cheddar cheese,
  grated

2 hard cooked eggs,
  chopped
½ cup tomato catsup
½ cup sweet pickle relish

Mix all ingredients well; store in refrigerator. If not to be used within two days, add eggs when ready to serve. Yields about 1 ½ pints.

THE SHAKER VILLAGE OF
PLEASANT HILL
Harrodsburg

IN THIS CHARMING COMmunity, twenty-seven 19th-century buildings have been restored on 2200 acres of beautiful rolling farmland, the largest and most complete of any Shaker colony still in existence.

A National Landmark from boundary to boundary, "Shakertown" was one of the most western and southern of the 18 Shaker communities founded during the late 18th and early 19th centuries.

The United Society of Believers in Christ's Second Appearing called themselves "Believers," but were known to outsiders as "Shakers" due to the dance-like form of their religious services. Individuals from many backgrounds gave up families and possessions to live apart from "the world" in an environment of sexual and racial equality. Shakers were celibate, industrious people, who dedicated their lives to hard work and superior craftsmanship. Their colony at Pleasant Hill endured a little over a hundred years, closing in 1910, and the last Kentucky Shaker died in 1923.

Many evidences of their work remain at Pleasant Hill today: original Shaker furniture, elegant and unornamented; hundreds of Shaker tools; and the buildings themselves, a simple, very Southern adaptation of Georgian Federal architecture.

In the restored buildings, interpreters in Shaker dress explain the strange, productive lives of the Shakers, and demonstrate spinning, quilting, hearth cooking, coopering, blacksmithing, and the making of the famous Shaker flat broom. During Shaker Heritage Weekends each September, additional programs of music, dance, cooking, and crafts are scheduled.

The serenity and calm of Shakertown may be enjoyed for an hour or two, overnight, or for days; lodging is available in fourteen of the historic buildings, with Shaker reproduction furniture in every room. From Shaker Landing, riverboat rides on The Dixie Belle offer a spectacular view of the Kentucky River's limestone cliffs.

Visitors have always been welcomed to the three-story brick Trustees' House. Electric candles gleam in cherry sconces suspended from Shaker peg-rails, simple muslin curtains tall windows, rag carpets cushion floors, and twin staircases spiral upward in simple beauty. In the dining rooms, Shaker-designed tables are bare, and the low chairs slide beneath with typical Shaker efficiency.

Regional Kentucky foods, seasonal favorites, and Shaker specialties are served at the table by waitresses in Shaker dress, with no limit to "helpings" of the delicious fresh vegtables.

Kitchen wizards, under the longtime direction of Elizabeth C. Kremer, also have a way with the hot breads featured at each meal, but starring at the lavish breakfast buffet. No one leaves Shakertown hungry; full though you may be, you are cautioned to "Shaker your plate," and like Pleasant Hill's original residents, leave nothing to waste.

The Shaker Village of Pleasant Hill Rte #4, Harrodsburg, KY 40330, (606)734-5411, is 25 miles southwest of Lexington via US 68, seven miles northeast of Harrodsburg. Three meals a day are served in seatings; reservations are strongly advised. Dress is casual, and there is a strict no-tipping policy. No charge cards are accepted. ($$)

PLEASANT HILL BREAKFAST SOUFFLÉ**

1½ pounds pork sausage
9 eggs, beaten slightly
3 cups milk
1½ teaspoons dry mustard
1 teaspoon salt
3 slices bread, cut in
⅛-inch cubes
1½ cups Cheddar cheese, grated

Brown sausage and drain. Spread in a 9" x 13" x 2" greased pan. Mix all other ingredients and spread over sausage; cover pan and refrigerate overnight. Bake uncovered for one hour at 350 degrees, and cut into squares to serve eight.

PLEASANT HILL SQUASH MUFFINS*

¾ cup brown sugar
¼ cup molasses
½ cup soft butter
1 egg, beaten
1 cup cooked, mashed
   squash
1 ¾ cups flour
1 teaspoon soda
¼ teaspoon salt
¼ cup pecans

Cream sugar, molasses and butter; add egg and squash and blend well. Mix flour with soda and salt and beat into squash batter. Fold in pecans. Fill well-greased muffin pans about half full; bake at 375 degrees for 20 minutes. Yields 1 ¼ dozen large muffins.

PLEASANT HILL POPCORN SOUP*

2 ½ cups fresh corn, cut off
    cobb and chopped
1 cup milk
3 tablespoons butter
½ medium onion, chopped
3 tablespoons flour

1 ½ teaspoons salt
Dash of pepper
2 ½ cups milk
½ cup half and half
Popcorn

Cook corn in 1 cup milk until tender. Melt butter and sauté onion until soft. Stir in flour, salt, and pepper, then additional milk, half and half, and cooked corn. Cook until thickened. Sprinkle top of soup with popcorn before serving. Serves four.

PLEASANT HILL OATMEAL PIE**

One 9-inch unbaked pie
    crust
¾ cup granulated sugar
6 Tablespoons butter
¾ cup corn syrup

2 eggs, beaten
1 teaspoon vanilla
¾ cup quick rolled oats
    uncooked

Mix together sugar, butter, and corn syrup. Fold in eggs, add vanilla and stir in oats. Pour into pie crust and bake at 350 degrees for 30 to 35 minutes. Serves eight.

---

* from WE MAKE YOU KINDLY WELCOME. by Elizabeth C. Kremer. Harrodsburg, Kentucky. Copyright © 1970. Used by permission.
** from WELCOME BACK TO PLEASANT HILL. by Elizabeth C. Kremer. Harrodsburg, Kentucky. Copyright © 1977. Used by permission.

BEAUMONT INN
Harrodsburg

THE OLDEST PERMANENT
settlement west of the Alleghenies, Harrodsburg was founded
in June, 1774. James Harrod and 30 companions had paddled
down the Monongahela and Ohio Rivers and up the Kentucky
River, then trekked overland to Big Spring, where they built
a fort.

Women and children arrived in the fall of 1775, bringing
civilization to the wilderness, and the outpost rapidly grew
into a gracious town, known for its culture and social life.

Among the many handsome Greek Revival structures remaining in Harrodsburg is white-columned Beaumont Inn,
built in the 1840's as a boarding school. Superior young ladies
knew it as Greenville Female Institute, Daughters' College,
and Beaumont College, all unusual institutions in which aca-
demically oriented curricula rivaled those in men's colleges
of the period.

The school continued in successful operation until 1914,
when its president and owner died. In 1918, Annie Bell God-
dard, a graduate of Daughters' College and former dean of
Beaumont College, opened Beaumont Inn, converting the college's spacious rooms into a country inn of great distinction.
Placed on the National Register of Historic Places in 1980,
it is now operated by the third and fourth generations of
her family.

Beaumont Inn is the focal point of 30 wooded acres; three
buildings on the grounds serve as additional guest houses,
and a total of twenty-nine rooms are filled with antiques,
many of which are family pieces. Here may be found the
relaxation and comfort of an earlier age, with the modern
pleasures of swimming, golf, and tennis.

Guests are welcomed to Beaumont Inn in a front hall filled
with memorabilia of General Robert E. Lee, and may meet
friends in a double parlor furnished with period antiques.
The reception area is in the former school library, in which
old books may still be seen. Large dining rooms in gold, green,
and pumpkin colors are settings for arrangements of fruits,
vegetables, and flowers, depending upon the season, but the
famous traditional Kentucky fare is the stellar attraction.

Fried "yellow-legged" chicken and carefully aged country ham top a menu of Southern favorites, and these, plus a daily special entrée, are accompanied by appetizer, salad, vegetables (including their renowned corn pudding), and homemade biscuits. Among old-fashioned dessert delights are their famous Robert E. Lee and Chocolate Sherry cakes, fruits in meringues and cobblers, Fig Pudding, and Huguenot Torte.

Beaumont Inn, 638 Beaumont Drive, Harrodsburg, Kentucky 40330, is open from the 2nd Thursday in March until December 15. Meals are served in seatings; breakfast is served only to over-night guests, and luncheon reservations are taken at 12 noon and 1:15, Monday through Saturday, 12 noon and 1:30 Sunday. Dinner is served at 6 and 7:15 p.m. Monday through Friday, 6 and 7:30 p.m. Saturday, and 6 p.m. only on Sunday. (606)734-3381. Harrodsburg is about 35 miles southwest of Lexington via US 68 or The Bluegrass Parkway and US 127. Dress code is informal; no shorts are allowed in the evenings. Reservations are advisable but not necessary except for Saturday evening, and there are reduced prices for children. V, MC. $$

BEAUMONT INN FROZEN FRUIT SALAD*

One 16-ounce can pineapple tidbits or chunks
One 16-ounce can fruit cocktail
One 6-ounce bottle maraschino cherries
12 ounces whipping cream

½ cup sugar
8 ounces cream cheese
½ cup mayonnaise
3 Tablespoons lemon juice
¼ teaspoon salt
3 medium bananas, sliced
Mayonnaise and parsley for garnish

Drain canned fruit well. Whip cream stiff; stir in sugar. Blend cream cheese with mayonnaise, lemon juice, and salt; add drained fruit, bananas, and whipped cream.

It is best to fill 3 cylindrical one-quart cardboard containers and freeze. These can be cut into 6 servings per carton. It can be frozen in plastic or glass containers, but is more trouble to serve.

Serve on lettuce leaf topped with mayonnaise and parsley. Serves 18.

BEAUMONT INN CARROT OR ASPARAGUS SOUFFLÉ*

1 cup cooked, ground
   carrots OR
1 cup asparagus pieces
1 Tablespoon flour
1 egg, beaten

1 ¼ cups milk
1 Tablespoon sugar
½ teaspoon salt
1 Tablespoon butter,
   melted

Mix carrots (or asparagus) with flour. Mix egg and milk, and combine the two mixtures. Add sugar, salt, and butter and stir well. Pour into buttered casserole, and bake at 375 degrees, stirring occasionally until mixture begins to thicken. Bake until firm but not dry.

BEAUMONT BRUNSWICK STEW*

2 ½ pound chicken
3 slices shoulder meat OR
6 slices bacon, diced
1 quart fresh or frozen lima
   beans
6 medium tomatoes, peeled
   and quartered
4 medium onions, peeled
   and quartered

6 medium potatoes, peeled
   and quartered
1 Tablespoon salt
1 teaspoon black pepper
1 teaspoon monosodium
   glutamate
4 ears corn, cut off cobb
   and scraped

In very large kettle, boil chicken and meat about 40 minutes in 1 ½ gallons of water. Remove from heat and strip chicken from bones back into kettle of liquid. Add another quart of water. Add other ingredients (except corn) and, stirring frequently, boil slowly for one hour. Add corn and continue to boil slowly another hour, stirring frequently to avoid scorching. Serve in bowl or over corn cakes, bread, or biscuits. Serves 20.

* from BEAUMONT INN SPECIAL RECIPES. Harrodsburg, Kentucky. Used by permission.

ELMWOOD INN
Perryville

Harberson's Fort, Es-

tablished before 1783 at the crossroads of the Danville-Louisville and Harrodsburg-Nashville routes, was renamed in 1815 for Commodore Perry, hero of the battle of Lake Erie. Laid out in a grid across the Chaplin River, Perryville grew equally on both sides. Stately Federal and Greek Revival houses nodded to each other across the river, and a row of riverfront shops in the Greek Revival style was built about 1840.

The peace of the little farming community was destroyed on October 8, 1862, when Confederate forces, led by General Braxton Bragg, and Union forces, under General Don Carlos Buell, collided just two miles away. More than 6,000 casualties resulted from one of the bloodiest battles of the War Between the States, and every available shelter became a makeshift hospital.

One of these is now Elmwood Inn. Since its construction in 1842, the Greek Revival house has also served as a residence, a co-educational private school, a music school, and an apartment building. It was restored in 1971, and is a Kentucky Landmark. With the rest of the Perryville Historic District, it was placed on the National Register of Historic Places in 1973.

Standing in a grove of maple and sweet gum trees overlooking the recently rechannelized Chaplin River, Elmwood Inn offers tradition-based food that owner Charles Bradshaw dubs "Kentucky Gourmet."

Upon entering the central hall, guests are immediately aware of the antiques and decorative elements which add to the atmosphere; a quaint Victorian parlor and two dining rooms, warmed by open fires in chilly weather, are visible through open doors. Upstairs dining rooms are equally comfortable, and warmweather guests may be seated on a shady terrace.

All meals feature chicken, "fried in a big black skillet" baked Kentucky ham, and chicken livers "Southern style." Lunch additions include "The Favorite," a soup-sandwich-salad combination, while the dinner menu adds a 10-ounce rib eye steak, baked Cornish hen, and a country ham/chicken combination. Homemade soups, special salads, country vegetables and marvelous hot breads (Portuguese Spice Bread!) are all noteworthy, but save room for ice cream with chocolate-bourbon sauce!

Elmwood Inn, 205 4th Street, Perryville, Kentucky 40468, is open from 12 Noon to 2 p.m. and 6 to 9 p.m., Tuesday through Saturday, and from 12 Noon to 8 p.m. on Sunday. (606)332-2271. Perryville is 9 miles from Danville via US 150 and 10 miles from Harrodsburg via US 68. Dress is casual, and reservations are requested; setups and glasses are provided for those who bring beverages. MC, V, personal checks. $$.

ELMWOOD INN ARTICHOKE AND SPINACH CASSEROLE

Four 10-ounce packages
chopped frozen spinach
Eleven ounces cream
cheese
5 Tablespoons melted
butter
Juice of 1 lemon
Two 16-ounce cans
artichoke hearts,
drained
Salt, pepper, and nutmeg

Cook spinach in boiling, salted water until thawed; drain well. Mix in cheese and butter until smooth. Add lemon juice, artichoke hearts and seasonings to taste. Place in casserole, cover with foil, and cut slits in foil to allow steam to escape. Bake at 350 degrees for 30 to 45 minutes. Serves six to eight.

ELMWOOD INN WEDDING RECEPTION PUNCH

One 12-ounce can frozen
lemonade
One 12-ounce can frozen
fruit punch
2 pints pineapple sherbet
Lemon slices and
Strawberries
One 28-ounce bottle ginger
ale

Dilute lemonade and fruit punch according to directions on cans. Combine in a large punch bowl, stirring in the softened sherbet. Float lemon slices and strawberries in the punch; just before serving, add ginger ale. Serves 25.

ELMWOOD INN'S DIRECTIONS FOR HOW TO COOK A COUNTRY HAM

Trim ham and wash thoroughly. Soak overnight in cold water; pour off water and cover ham with fresh cold water. Place container on stove and bring water to boil. Add ½ cup cloves and ½ cup vinegar to water. Boil 15 minutes per pound of ham. Remove ham from water and allow to cool; remove skin and place ham with fat side up. Pat with ½ cup brown sugar and bake at 400 degrees for 45 minutes or until brown on top.

ELMWOOD INN SUMMER SQUASH CASSEROLE

1 pound yellow summer
  squash
1 medium onion
2 Tablespoons butter
3 Tablespoons flour
1 cup milk
4 ounces sharp American
  cheese

One 3-ounce can sliced
  mushrooms, drained
½ cup soft breadcrumbs
¼ cup chopped pecans,
  sautéed in
1 Tablespoon melted butter

Slice squash and onion ¼ inch thick. Cook in boiling, salted water until tender; drain. In saucepan, melt 2 tablespoons butter; blend in flour. Add milk; cook and stir until thick. Add cheese and mushrooms; stir until cheese is melted. Arrange half of vegetables in 1 ½ quart casserole, cover with half of sauce, then repeat. Bake, covered, at 350 degrees for 25 minutes. Sprinkle with pecan mixture; bake, uncovered, 20 to 25 minutes longer. Serves six to eight.

HOLLY HILL INN
Midway

SOME OF THE MOST BEAU-

tiful horse country in the world may be found in Woodford County, Kentucky—black or white plank fences and hand-stacked gray stone walls border lush green fields where horses graze contentedly, and spacious Colonial homes are glimpsed through sheltering trees. This area typifies what many people think of when they hear the word "Kentucky."

Shady lanes through the gently rolling countryside lead to the county seat, Versailles (pronounced Ver-SALES) and to the little railroad village of Midway. Called "The first town in Kentucky built by a railroad," Midway has changed little since 1832; it still has tracks down the middle of its main street, now lined with specialty shops in historic buildings. Comfortable Victorian-era houses surround the "downtown," and the entire town is on the National Register of Historic Places.

The house that was to become Holly Hill Inn was built in 1850, on the site of an early stagecoach inn that burned. Enlarged and remodeled in the late 1890's, when the graceful bowed Classical Revival porch was added, it was made an inn in 1979 by Rex and Rose Lyons, who preserve "the feeling of dining in someone's home." In addition to the restaurant, three rooms are maintained for overnight guests.

Some of the furniture in the house "has always been here," Rex said, indicating an elaborate overmantel in the library, similar to one in Charles Dickens' house in England; a handsome Kentucky walnut corner cupboard in the main dining room; and a half-canopy bed in one of the guest rooms. Additional antiques, old brass, the Greek Revival cherry woodwork, and restrained decorating in a scheme of Empire green contribute to a comfortable, relaxing environment.

Holly Hill's menu changes according to availability of fresh ingredients, but favorite offerings recur in the cozy dining rooms. Among these are Chicken Breast with Sauce Louie, Baked Country Ham, Grilled Salmon with Cucumber sauce, and Marinated Beef Tenderloin. Seasonally, lamb, seafood and veal entrées join the list. All are served with soup, salad, beautifully prepared vegetables, and homemade hot breads. Desserts vary also, and are inevitably special.

Holly Hill Inn, North Winter Street, Midway, Kentucky 40347, is open 11:30 a.m. to 2:30 p.m., and 5:30 to 9:30 p.m., Monday through Saturday, and from 12 Noon to 2 p.m. on Sunday. (606)846-4732. The inn is closed for the month of February. Midway is 12 miles west of Lexington via I-64 or US 421. Dress is informal, and dinner is by reservation only; wine is served. No charge cards are accepted. ($$)

HOLLY HILL INN CHESS CAKES

1 pound light brown sugar
1 cup white sugar
4 eggs
1 cup butter
2 cups flour
3 teaspoons baking powder
1 teaspoon salt
1 teaspoon vanilla
½ cup chopped pecans

Combine sugars, eggs, and butter; beat until light. Sift together flour, baking powder, and salt, and add to egg mixture, blending well. Add vanilla and nuts, and pour into greased and floured 9 ½" x 13 ½" pan. Bake at 325 degrees for 45 to 50 minutes or until firm around edges; center should remain soft. Cut into approximately 1-inch squares to serve— these are extremely rich. Makes over a hundred tiny squares.

HOLLY HILL INN HAM SPREAD

¼ cup mayonnaise
2 Tablespoons prepared
  mustard
2 Tablespoons
  Worcestershire sauce
2 teaspoons chili powder
½ teaspoon paprika
1 Tablespoon (or more)
  chopped onion
1 cup ground cooked ham
  (country ham is not
  suitable)

Combine all ingredients except ham, and mix well, then add ham. Serve with crackers or as a sandwich filling. An excellent use for leftover ham.

HOLLY HILL INN MOLDED GAZPACHO SALAD

1 ½ Tablespoons
unflavored gelatin
1 ½ cup tomato juice
1 cucumber, peeled and
finely chopped
4 large tomatoes, peeled
and finely chopped
1 large green pepper, finely
chopped
¼ cup sliced radishes
2 Tablespoons green onion,
finely chopped

½ cup celery, finely
chopped
Dash of hot sauce
¼ cup olive oil
1 ½ Tablespoons wine
vinegar
1 Tablespoon lemon juice
1 teaspoon salt
Creamy dressing (see
below)

Soften gelatin in ¼ cup cold water and set aside. Heat tomato juice in a large saucepan; add gelatin and stir until dissolved. Add vegetables and seasonings; mix well, and chill until slightly thickened. Stir well, and pour into oiled 6-cup mold. Chill until firm; unmold and serve with creamy dressing. Serves eight to ten.

Creamy dressing:

½ cup mayonnaise
½ cup commercial sour
cream

¾ cup fresh parsley,
minced

Combine all ingredients, mixing well. Yields about 1 ¼ cups.

SCIENCE HILL INN
Shelbyville

WHEN JULIA ANN TEVIS

moved to Shelbyville with her Methodist clergyman husband in 1824, she opened Science Hill Female Academy, a school for girls which offered a real curriculum. The school was not expected to succeed—young ladies were considered to have little need of "boys' subjects:" chemistry, mathematics, history, botany, rhetoric, and philosophy.

Nevertheless, 20 students appeared on the first day, and immediate expansion began. A large dining room, dormitory and class rooms and a chapel were added, for a total of 78 rooms surrounding a courtyard, which was enclosed in 1848.

By that time, there were more than 200 day and boarding pupils, from many states, and John Tevis had given up the ministry to become spiritual head of the school. Science Hill continued in operation until 1939 with only one change in ownership, maintaining an outstanding reputation for education.

The building was used for a time as a residential inn, and in 1947, Mark Scearce opened Wakefield-Scearce Galleries in the chapel, showing antiques, silver, and decorative accessories. In 1960, he bought the entire structure, and today the internationally known gallery shares the former school, a Kentucky Landmark on the National Register, with six specialty shops and the popular restaurant, Science Hill Inn.

Under the management of Terry and Donna Gill since 1978, food at Science Hill Inn takes traditional Kentucky fare a logical step forward. "We're trying to give people a taste of Kentucky," Chef Donna said. "People are more sophisticated and more knowledgeable, so we try to upgrade a little, substituting fresh ingredients whenever possible."

Entering through the glass-roofed courtyard, guests step down into the high-ceilinged Georgian dining room, where good food has been served for 150 years. Tall windows on two sides overlook shady old gardens, and fresh flowers and white linens gleam in the sunlight. Here are presented Kentucky Bibb lettuce salad (with artichoke hearts, turkey, cheese, and country ham), or Kentucky trout, chicken, steaks, country ham, special salads and elegant sandwiches, plus a choice of rich homemade desserts.

The Sunday buffet, served on silver from the Wakefield-Scearce vault, always offers fried chicken, country ham, and barbecued brisket of beef with corn pudding and country-style green beans, and may include zucchini casserole, cauliflower with mustard mayonnaise, tomato pudding, cucumber mousse, and wild rice salad, with buttermilk biscuits and hot water cornbread. This is Kentucky hospitality at its best, and there's still dessert. . . .

Science Hill Inn, 525 Washington Street, Shelbyville, Kentucky 40065, is open only for lunch, from 11:30 a.m. to 2:30 p.m., Tuesday through Saturday, and from 11:30 a.m. to 2:30 p.m. for the Sunday buffet. It is closed the second and third weeks in February. (502)633-2825. Shelbyville is about 45 miles west of Lexington, 28 miles east of Louisville, via US 60 or I-64. Dress is casual, beer and wine are available, and reservations are suggested. AE, MC, V. ($$)

SCIENCE HILL INN CREAM OF CABBAGE SOUP*

6 slices bacon, diced
1 head cabbage, shredded
1 medium onion, chopped
2 quarts chicken stock
1 cup heavy cream
Grated Swiss cheese

In large pot, fry bacon until crisp; remove bacon and set aside. To bacon grease in pot, add cabbage and onion; cook until limp, stirring occasionally. Do not let it brown. Add stock and simmer until vegetables are tender.

Remove from heat and purée in blender. Return to pot, add cream, and garnish with bacon and grated cheese. Serves ten.

SCIENCE HILL INN CUCUMBER MOUSSE*

2 Tablespoons plain
   gelatin
1 medium cucumber
2 cups mayonnaise
1 ½ cups sour cream
2 teaspoons salt
2 Tablespoons dill weed
2 Tablespoons lemon juice

In a saucepan, sprinkle gelatin over ½ cup water and set aside. Peel, seed, and shred cucumber and place in mixing bowl. Add remaining ingredients except gelatin, and mix well.

Over low heat dissolve gelatin and add to cucumber mixture. Pour into oiled 1 ½ quart mold and chill until set.

SCIENCE HILL INN BUTTERMILK BISCUITS*

2 ½ cups flour
2 teaspoons baking powder
½ teaspoon baking soda
1 teaspoon salt
½ cup shortening, plus 2 tablespoons
¾ cup buttermilk

Sift dry ingredients. Cut in shortening until it resembles coarse meal; stir in milk. Knead lightly on floured board. Roll out ½-inch thick, cut and place on buttered pan. Bake at 375 degrees for 15 minutes.

SCIENCE HILL INN BROWN SUGAR PIE*

One 9-inch unbaked pie shell
1 pound light brown sugar
4 Tablespoons flour
3 eggs
¾ cup melted butter
¾ cup half and half cream
Whipped cream for topping

In mixing bowl, combine sugar and flour. Beat in eggs one at a time. Gradually add butter and cream and mix until well combined. Pour into pie shell and bake at 350 degrees for 40 to 50 minutes. Serve warm, topped with lightly sweetened whipped cream. Serves eight.

* from *DONNA GILL RECOMMENDS*. Shelbyville, Kentucky. Used by permission.

OLD STONE INN
Simpsonville

As EARLY AS THE 1770'S, settlers attempted to make their homes in what is now Shelby County. The beautiful, thickly wooded countryside, abundant water, and reasonable proximity to the settlement at the Falls of the Ohio (now Louisville) made it seem an ideal location. Native Americans had other ideas, however, and the area was the site of bloody massacres and attacks.

The earliest successful fort was established by Squire Boone in 1779 at The Painted Stone. It was abandoned briefly after repeated Indian attacks but was reoccupied, and remained under Boone's charge until he left to take his seat in the Virginia Legislature in 1783.

Rich in history and legend, Shelby County is now known as one of the dairy and Burley tobacco centers of Kentucky, and also enjoys a reputation for excellence in the production of Saddlebred horses.

Harking back to that time when determined pioneers established themselves, Old Stone Inn is popularly believed to have bankrupted its original owner, Fleming P. Rogers, who built it as a residence, but sold it before it was completed. Original oak and poplar floors, fireplaces in each room, and a spacious hall confirm that the house was built of the finest materials, and the massive stone walls show that protection was still needed.

Its eleven rooms have been increased by harmonious additions on either end, which accommodate today's crowds without losing the feeling of a more spacious era. A Kentucky Landmark, the building was placed on The National Register in 1976.

Old Stone Inn was a stagecoach stop on the Lexington-Louisville Pike for many years, and was re-opened as a restaurant in 1924 after use as a residence. Antique furnishings add to the homelike atmosphere, and traditional Kentucky foods are served family style by present owner Bill Fensterer, who has operated the restaurant since 1969.

Open April through November, Old Stone Inn serves meals Wednesday through Saturday evenings and Sunday mid-day. Entrées of chicken, ham, seafood, beef, and chicken and ham combinations are listed in the hall in the Southern manner.

Included in each meal are choices of soup, salad, main course, beverage and dessert. The inn's famed stuffed eggplant, corn pudding, green beans, potatoes, and other vegetables (for a total of four at any meal) and hot breads are passed at the table. Everything is homemade, portions are generous, and you'll take away a bit of the Old South in your memory.

The Old Stone Inn, Simpsonville, Kentucky 40347, is open April through November for dinner only, Wednesday through Saturday from 5:30 to 8 p.m., and on Sunday from 12:30 to 7:30 p.m. (502)722-8882. Dress is informal, and reservations are preferred. AE, CB, DC, MC, V. ($$)

OLD STONE INN CORN FRITTERS

6 eggs
12 ounces milk
1 ½ pounds flour
½ ounce salt
1 ½ ounces baking powder
½ ounce sugar
1 ounce cooking oil
2 ½ pounds canned whole
    kernel corn, drained
Deep fat for frying
Powdered sugar

In large bowl, beat eggs, add milk, and blend well.

Sift flour, salt, baking powder and sugar together. Add to milk mixture, and beat smooth. Beat in cooking oil, then corn, and stir until well blended.

Drop tablespoons of the batter into deep fat and brown for 2 to 3 minutes. Roll in powdered sugar and serve while hot. Yields about 25 fritters.

OLD STONE INN SCALLOPED ZUCCHINI

4 large zucchini, cut into
    ½-inch round slices
4 hard-cooked eggs,
    chopped
One 10 ¾-ounce can
    condensed Cheddar
    cheese soup
⅓ cup heavy cream
½ cup grated sharp
    Cheddar cheese
¼ cup seasoned dry bread
    crumbs

Layer zucchini and eggs alternately in a greased 8-inch square pan, ending with eggs. Mix soup and cream; spoon evenly over casserole, and sprinkle top with grated cheese and crumbs. Bake at 350 degrees 40 to 45 minutes, or until zucchini is easily pierced with a fork and the top of the casserole is lightly browned. Serves six.

OLD STONE INN STUFFED EGGPLANT

1 large eggplant
½ teaspoon salt
¼ cup chopped onion
1 Tablespoon butter
One 10 ½-ounce can
   condensed cream of
   mushroom soup

1 teaspoon Worcestershire
   sauce
1 cup fine cracker crumbs
1 Tablespoon chopped
   parsley

Slice off one side of eggplant and remove pulp to within ½ inch of skin. Dice removed pulp; place in saucepan with ½ cup water and salt, and simmer until tender. Drain.

In skillet, sauté onion in butter, and stir into eggplant with soup, Worcestershire sauce, and all but 2 tablespoons of the cracker crumbs. Fill eggplant shell with the mixture, and place in shallow pan; top with reserved crumbs and parsley.

Pour 1 ½ cups water into pan around eggplant, and bake at 375 degrees for one hour. Serves four.

TRATTORIA MATTEI
Middletown

On a Pleasant Knoll

overlooking US 60, the country residence of a Louisville mantel manufacturer is now an Italian trattoria (pronounced tra-toe-REE-ya), or inn, providing a change from the more expected flavors of Kentucky. Probably built about 1898, the house is an uncommon style for the area; large and square, with wide verandahs and high ceilings, it has a feeling of the Deep South, leading to speculation that it may have been a summer home.

During restoration in the early 1970's, layers of paint were stripped from woodwork, and when one mantel was removed from the wall, the name "Hegan Mantel and Woodworking Company" was found on the back. The property had belonged to E.C. Hegan, treasurer of that company, who died in 1909, and an interurban stop at the entrance was called "Hegan Station."

Mantles, trim, and doors are of a different wood in each room and the wide central hall; tiger-striped cherry, mahogany, and oak are used. Although adaptation for restaurant use has enclosed one side of the verandah, the woodwork has been carefully matched. Added embellishments are an interesting sidelight: the family of owner/chef Dominick Mattei has been in the business of making plaster rosettes and motifs for generations in Italy, and in Louisville since 1921. Several decorate walls and ceilings in the restaurant.

Depending upon the weather, dinner guests are seated in firelit dining rooms on two floors or on the verandah; strolling musicians serenade on weekends and other special occasions.

Mattei, an engineer whose maternal grandparents owned a restaurant in Italy, realized a lifetime dream when he opened Trattoria Mattei on Columbus Day, 1972. He follows their philosophy: "Give people good food and plenty of it and they'll keep coming back," and his Seven Course Original Italian Feast stems from a family reunion in Italy in 1961. This "Pranzo" is an all-you-can-eat banquet, and can fill several hours with delicious samplings of classic Italian cuisine.

Additional menu choices include 12 antipasti, and pasta, veal, beef, seafood and chicken entrées. Special Italian meats are flown in from Massachusetts, veal is purchased by the ton, and although sauces are prepared in huge quantities, recipes are the same savory combinations used in the Mattei home. Among the unusual desserts is a sherbet-stuffed orange, drenched with cordial: most refreshing after a hearty meal!

Trattoria Mattei, 15206 Shelbyville Road, Anchorage, Kentucky 40223, is on US 60, 1 ¼ miles east of the Jefferson Freeway, off I-65 just east of Louisville (502)245-3333. It is open for dinner only, Tuesday through Saturday from 5 to 10:30 p.m., and all beverages and a large selection of Italian wines are served. Dress is informal, and reservations are preferred, especially on weekends. AE, MC, V ($$).

TRATTORIA MATTEI MEAT SAUCE FOR PASTA

3 medium onions, chopped
3 strips celery, chopped
2 carrots, chopped
Olive oil for sautéeing
1 pound lean ground round
1 clove garlic, minced
One 20-ounce can whole tomatoes
Salt and pepper
1 Tablespoon dried basil
One 6-ounce can tomato paste

In large pot, sauté vegetables in olive oil; set aside. In skillet, fry ground round with garlic, add to vegetables and stir to blend. Add tomatoes, breaking by squeezing tomatoes in your hand. Simmer about 1 ½ hours, or until tomatoes are done. Add seasonings; about 20 minutes before serving, add tomato paste. Simmer until ready to serve, check seasoning, and serve on pasta prepared according to package directions. Serves six.
Note: One pound pasta serves 5 people if there are additional courses; use 1 ½ pounds if pasta is only dish served.

TRATTORIA MATTEI VEAL PARMESAN

1 ½ pounds veal scallops
Flour, seasoned with salt and pepper
1 egg, beaten with
1 Tablespoon milk
Bread or cracker crumbs
Dried parsley, pepper, and granulated garlic
Grated Parmesan cheese
Marinara sauce (see below)
Sliced mozzarella cheese

Dredge veal in seasoned flour, then dip in egg-milk mixture, then in crumbs seasoned with parsley, pepper, and garlic. Sprinkle with grated cheese. In skillet, sauté scallops; arrange in a baking dish and top with marinara sauce. Place a slice of mozzarella on each piece of veal, and bake at 350 degrees until cheese melts and browns in a few spots. Serves six.

For marinara sauce:

3 medium onions, chopped
3 strips celery, chopped
2 carrots, chopped
Olive oil
One 20-ounce can whole
    tomatoes
Salt and pepper

1 Tablespoon dried sweet
    basil
1 ½ teaspoons dried
    oregano
One 6-ounce can tomato
    paste

Sauté vegetables in olive oil; add tomatoes, breaking by squeezing tomatoes in your hand. Allow to simmer about 1 ½ hours, until tomatoes are cooked. Add seasonings, and about 20 minutes before serving, add tomato paste. Simmer until ready to serve, and check for seasoning.

TRATTORIA MATTEI ARANCIONE di MATTEI

6 large California navel
    oranges
½ gallon orange sherbet

Amaretto, Grand Marnier,
    or any
liqueur compatible with
    orange)

Slice off tops of oranges, about ⅜ inch, and reserve. With a sharp pointed knife, cut a cone-shaped wedge out of the center of each orange, being careful not to pierce bottom. With a tablespoon, sever the orange sections from the white membrane, scraping the shell clean. Freeze shells and caps. Squeeze orange juice from pulp, reserving for another use, and add pulp to slightly softened orange sherbet, mixing well. Freeze sherbet mixture overnight, then fill each orange shell, mounding sherbet mixture slightly. Top with caps and freeze until ready to serve. To serve, remove caps, pierce center of sherbet and fill with liqueur; replace tops and serve in small dishes. Paper doily will keep orange steady in dish. Serves six.

THE UNICORN TEA ROOM
Jeffersontown

EARLY SETTLERS OF THE

area now called Jeffersontown were three Tyler brothers, Robert, Moses, and Ned, who built a log and stone house about 1771; Captain Robert Tyler was the great, great grandfather of President Harry S. Truman.

Others followed, finding good hunting, abundant water, and fertile soil. The settlement of "Bruner's Town," named for another pioneer, was re-named in honor of Vice President Thomas Jefferson in 1797, when streets were laid out and lots sold.

A lot on Main Street (now Watterson Trail) at College Drive was sold to William and Valentine Conrad, who operated a nearby pottery. According to local tradition, they constructed a two-story house of massive logs on a stone foundation, with a one-story, one-room ell at the rear, forming the first section of a house that grew with subsequent owners.

Dr. John Simpson Seaton, a professor at the Kentucky School of Medicine, bought the property in 1844 and doubled the size of the house during the ten years he owned it. Two other doctors, Samuel B. Mills and Samuel N. Marshall, lived in the house in sequence. The property remained in the Marshall family until 1964, and the front facade is believed to have been rebuilt about 1900 by Dr. Marshall's heirs. The house has been named a Kentucky Landmark.

When Mary Kay App opened an interior design studio in the house in the mid-1960's, she named the business for Dr. Seaton, and Seaton House Galleries has been an important resource for decorative design ever since. A workroom addition with large windows was converted to a tearoom in 1983, the skylit second floor serving as a private reception room.

In early 1985, Bob Reid, of Reid's Food Service, Inc., a volume catering operation, acquired The Unicorn Tea Room as a showcase for the products of his organization.

The bright, cheerful room, decorated in shades of deep green, with a mural of mother and child unicorns, offers tearoom food Reid patterns after that of a fine Canadian hotel. Lunch is light and flavorful, with delicate soups and entrées, Olive Nut Cheese on Brown Bread, or Chicken Breast Salad on a croissant. There's a Chef's Salad full of artichokes, asparagus, and strips of ham and cheese; and Chocolate Mousse Pie (with a chocolate crunch crust) or blueberry pie for dessert.

Afternoon Tea with finger sandwiches, crumpets and fruit preserves provides iced tea in summer, and a choice of hot Bigelow teas in winter. The Unicorn is truly a Tearoom!

The Unicorn Tea Room, 10320 Watterson Trail, Jeffersontown, Kentucky 40299, is open for lunch from 11:30 a.m. to 2:30 p.m. and for Afternoon Tea from 3 to 4 p.m., Monday through Friday. Dress is casual, reservations are appreciated, and no charge cards are accepted. ($)

UNICORN DRINK

6 ounces pineapple juice
⅛ of a honeydew melon, peeled and cubed

Juice of ½ lemon
1 cup crushed ice

In a blender, place juice, melon cubes, lemon juice and ice. Blend for 10 seconds, and serve at once. Serves one.

UNICORN TEA ROOM BROCCOLI SOUP

Two 10-ounce packages frozen chopped broccoli
2 quarts chicken broth
1 cup instant potato flakes
3 cups non-dairy liquid creamer

1 Tablespoon salt
4 ounces (1 stick) butter
Parmesan cheese

In large pot, place broccoli in broth and cook until tender. Add remaining ingredients, and simmer 10 to 15 minutes. Sprinkle Parmesan cheese over each serving. Yields 3 quarts.

UNICORN TEA ROOM CHICKEN SALAD

1 pound chicken breast, cut in ¼-inch cubes
¼ pound pickle relish
1 Tablespoon pimientoes, chopped

¼ teaspoon white pepper
1 teaspoon salt
2 teaspoons chicken soup base mix*
1 pint sour cream

In large bowl, mix chicken, relish, and pimientoes. In another bowl, mix white pepper, salt, and chicken soup base into the sour cream, and let the mixture rest five minutes or long enough to absorb the chicken flavoring. Then blend this with the chicken mixture.

Note: The chicken soup base is a commercial mixture available to restaurants; the home cook might try a small amount of chicken bouillon, reducing or eliminating the salt. Bouillon is sometimes quite salty.

CARROLLTON INN
Carrollton

THE POINT AT WHICH THE

Kentucky river flows into the Ohio was an important landing place during Kentucky's early years. Indians knew the beautiful valley for its good hunting, and the rivers for transportation through the dense forest.

James McBride, traveling by canoe from Pittsburg, carved his name into a tree about 1754, and is believed to have been the first white man in this part of the country. Simon Kenton came to hunt and stayed a few months, and James Harrod and his group stopped on their way to settle Harrodsburg in 1774. The point was permanently settled in 1790, when General (later Governor) Charles Scott and his Kentucky Volunteers built a blockhouse. Families who settled then are still represented in the area, and enjoy some of the loveliest scenery in the state.

The little settlement, first called Port William, was renamed when the county was re-divided in 1838, and county and county seat were named for Charles Carroll of Carrollton, Maryland, a signer of the Declaration of Independence.

Carrollton's most prosperous years came with the growth of river traffic. By 1794 there was regular boat traffic out of Pittsburgh on the Ohio, with the journey to Louisville requiring ten days, to New Orleans, 75 days. Despite Indian ambush and river disasters, the romantic riverboat era had begun; thousands earned their living on the Ohio, and to even greater numbers, the river was the highway to a new land.

Colorful river people, ranging from raftsmen and flatboat men to captains of luxury steamboats, found Carrollton a pleasant place to stop. Riverboat captains established comfortable homes and private clubs, and Houghton House was built in 1884 as a fine hotel catering to steamboat passengers. Three stories high, with comfortable guest rooms and a gracious dining room, the sturdy brick structure faced the Ohio river across a shady street.

Following several lean years, the building was restored in 1982, and is once again known for fine dining—now as The Carrollton Inn. Travelers from Indianapolis, Louisville and Cincinnati come by road and river, some just to dine, while others stay several days to visit the historic town, placed on the National Register in 1982, or to ski or enjoy summer recreation at nearby General Butler State Park.

Overnight rooms were reduced to ten as dining space grew to accommodate visitors who enjoy the 1880's atmosphere and good food served three times daily. Owner-chef Bob Rice, formerly in the wholesale meat business, believes his restaurant's popularity is based on quality and consistency. "I know what and where to buy meats and can tell the quality," he said. "I buy the very best."

Breakfast, at The Carrollton Inn, is served anytime—'We pride ourselves on our sausage gravy and biscuits," Rice says— but the menu provides choices to suit almost anyone.

Begin with the rich clam chowder, a favorite for miles around, then enjoy the salad bar, included with all dinners, and with specials such as Chicken with Country (or city) Ham au Gratin, Veal Parmesan, White Fish au Gratin, open faced Roast Beef, and "good old fashioned country ham on toast smothered in red-eye gravy."

The Light Lunch platter features ham, chicken, or tuna salad, and there are special burgers and more than a dozen sandwiches. Entrées include prime and choice beef, seafood, chicken, chicken livers, and ham. For those with the capacity, there are several fruit pies, carrot cake, and ice creams and sherbets.

Carrollton Inn, 218 Main Street (corner of 3rd), Carrollton, Kentucky 41008, is open 6 a.m. to 11 p.m. Monday through Saturday, and from 8 a.m. to 10 p.m. Sunday, with continuous service. (502)732-6905. Carrollton is about 45 miles northeast of Louisville, about 60 miles southwest of Cincinnati, just 2 miles from I-71 on the Ohio River. Dress is casual, all beverages are served, and reservations are preferred and probably necessary on weekends, for groups of six or more, or for overnight guests. AE, MC, V. ($$)

CARROLLTON INN CLAM CHOWDER

1 ½ pounds chopped clams   2 quarts milk, boiling
½ pound butter   Salt and white pepper
1 pound flour (about 3 ½
   cups)

In large pot, place clams with 2 or 3 quarts water, bring to boil, and simmer about one hour or until done.

In very large pot over medium heat melt butter; blend in flour and remove from heat. Pour in boiling milk and stir until blended. Mixture will be very thick.

Pour clams with their broth into milk mixture, stir to blend, and heat 45 minutes to one hour. Do not boil. Add salt and white pepper to taste, and serve with oyster crackers. Yields about one gallon.

CARROLLTON INN CHICKEN AND HAM AU GRATIN

6 ounces country ham, sliced
3 ounces baked chicken breast, sliced

1 slice bread, toasted
Cream sauce (see note)
Parmesan cheese, grated
Paprika

Fry ham quickly in its own grease.

In ovenproof dish, place toast; top with fried ham, sliced chicken breast, and enough cream sauce to cover well. Sprinkle heavily with Parmesan cheese and paprika, and broil 30 seconds to one minute, or until brown. Serves one.

Note: a medium cream sauce may be made of 1 ½ Tablespoons flour, 1 ½ Tablespoons butter, and 1 cup hot milk, cooked together over medium heat until thickened. Mr. Rice seasons his with a commercial chicken base available to restaurants; the home cook might try a small amount of chicken bouillon, using caution: bouillon is sometimes salty, and the country ham is very salty already.

THE ROBIN'S NEST
LaGrange

In 1824, OLDHAM COUNTY
was formed from parts of Jefferson, Shelby, and Henry counties. It was named for Colonel William Oldham, a Revolutionary soldier who commanded a regiment of Kentucky militia, and was killed in 1791 at Saint Clair's defeat, an ill-fated Indian campaign on the Wabash River.

The engaging little town of LaGrange, the county seat, is the birthplace of film pioneer D.W. Griffith, and also of the founder of the Order of the Eastern Star. It has long been a "bedroom town" for those who appreciate small town life yet work in Louisville.

One factor that made this kind of commuting feasible was the interurban railway, a phenomenon of the late 19th and early 20th centuries, which reached its peak just before World War I. Thriving in the states of Ohio, Indiana, Illinois, and Michigan, interurban lines utilized electric traction cars— like long distance streetcars with heavier, faster bodies—and connected towns by public transportation.

Indianapolis was considered the hub of eastern interurbans, and Louisville was a nearby center. The Louisville and Eastern Railroad had lines to such outlying towns as Okalona, Pleasure Ridge, Glenview, and Shelbyville.

The line, which had ended in Anchorage in 1901, was extended to LaGrange in 1907, and a station was built for passengers and freight. This was the end of the line, where the car turned around for its return trip.

Like other interurbans, the Louisville and Eastern succumbed to competition from automobiles, and disappeared as rapidly as it had spread. The abandoned LaGrange station housed several businesses before Robin and Pam Horn decided it should become the restaurant they had planned for four years.

Three months of removing partitions, painting and cleaning, and The Robin's Nest opened, in November of 1983. By April of 1984, Robin was chief cook, while Pam made soups, salads, and pies. It's a genuine family operation, and that gives The Robin's Nest a personal touch. "I fix everything just like I'd be eating it myself," Robin said.

Guests are served in the former waiting room near a potbellied stove, or in an ice-house turned loft, surrounded by crafts, period art, and old waybills found in the station. Pam's soups—cream of cauliflower and clam chowder are favorites—are almost a meal in themselves; other treats include Robin's Special Sandwich (ham and melted cheese, topped with bacon and tomato), savory baked filet of cod, and homemade Chicken Cordon Bleu. Extra special desserts are the copyrighted Kentucky Silk Pie, with a meringue crust, and Chocolate Eclair Mousse.

The Robin's Nest, 204 West Main Street, LaGrange, Kentucky 40031, is open for lunch Monday through Saturday, from 11 a.m. to 3 p.m., and for dinner Thursday through Saturday, from 5 to 10 p.m. in summer, to 9 p.m. in winter. (502)222-9581. Dress is casual, and reservations are preferred for ten people or more, and requested during October, November, and December. MC, V. ($$)

ROBIN'S NEST VEGETABLE PIE

One 9-inch unbaked pie
  shell
3 eggs
⅔ cup milk
½ teaspoon salt

1 cup cooked broccoli
½ cup sautéed onions and
  mushrooms, combined
1 tomato, sliced

Place pie shell on oven rack. Beat eggs, milk and salt together; add vegetables, and pour into pie shell.

Bake at 400 degrees for 35 minutes. Before removing from oven, place tomato slices on top, and bake an additional five minutes. Serves four.

ROBIN'S NEST CREAMY CHICKEN
NOODLE SOUP

½ fryer chicken
3 quarts water
3 ribs celery, chopped
10 mushrooms, sliced
3 carrots, chopped
2 ounces chopped onion
One 2-ounce jar pimientos

2 cups small egg noodles
Salt and pepper
4 ounces (½ stick) butter
2 cups milk
1 Tablespoon cornstarch,
  optional

In large pot, cook chicken in water until done. Remove chicken, pull meat from bones into small chunks, discard skin and bones, and return meat to pot. Add vegetables, and cook over medium heat about 30 minutes; add noodles and cook an additional ten minutes. Season with salt and pepper; add butter and milk. If thickening is needed, mix cornstarch with a little water and stir into soup. Heat through and serve.

ROBIN'S NEST CHOCOLATE ECLAIR MOUSSE

Graham crackers
Two 3 ¾-ounce boxes
    French Vanilla Instant
    Pudding mix
3 cups cold milk
8 ounces whipped topping,
    thawed
1 Tablespoon rum extract

2 ½ ounces unsweetened
    chocolate
1 ½ sticks margarine
2 teaspoons vanilla
1 ½ cups powdered sugar
2 Tablespoons light corn
    syrup
3 Tablespoons milk

Line 8″ x 12″ or 9″ x 13″ pan with whole Graham crackers.

In bowl, mix pudding with milk until thickened, add whipped topping, and flavor with rum extract. Layer pudding mixture and Graham crackers, ending with crackers. Set aside.

In saucepan, melt chocolate and margarine over low heat. Stir in vanilla, powdered sugar, corn syrup, and milk, and blend thoroughly. Place in refrigerator briefly to thicken.

Spread chocolate mixture on top layer of Graham crackers and place completed dish in refrigerator for at least 12 hours Cut into squares to serve.

JOHN E's
Louisville

Revolutionary War

hero George Hikes received land grants in Kentucky and settled near Louisville; his substantial acreage was later divided among his sons, and several of their houses still exist. One structure, believed to have been built about 1851 on the site of an earlier house, was a simple log cabin of two rooms downstairs and two up, with a dogtrot hall between.

The rough character of interior materials, recently exposed, leads to speculation that the house may have been built earlier for use as an outbuilding, and converted to a dwelling when the main house burned—walls of the house were constructed from hewn logs 14 to 18 inches wide. Outer walls were covered with clapboard and inner ones plastered, and although some additons were made, the house was relatively unchanged when it passed out of the Hikes family in 1947. A nearby cemetery contains graves of several members of this prominent Louisville family, and the house is a Kentucky Landmark.

It became a restaurant in the 1950's, and by that time, the city had grown up around it; the building had been expanded by further additions. Renovation has exposed the logs on some interior walls, and the four original rooms are now the core of a rambling restaurant which took its name, John E's, from two of the owners. It has been run by John and Penny Shanchuck and Ben and Barbara Edelen since 1983.

A patio, added in 1984, was so successful that it has been enclosed for year-round use, providing an alternative ambiance and a setting for live entertainment on weekends.

John E's serves what its owners describe as "good old American food," comprised of such diverse items as Kentucky burgoo (a traditional stew), their very special steaks, and selections like rumaki, mahi-mahi, and celestial chicken, which remain from John Shanchuck's tenure at a Polynesian restaurant. All are made from scratch every day.

The lunch menu offers salads, sandwiches, and lighter entrees, while dinner specialties from the charcoal broiler include barbecued baby ribs, a steak and lobster combination, and the two-pound T-bone. Among desserts are homemade cheesecake and marvelous homemade black bottom pie.

John E's Restaurant, 3708 Bardstown Road, Louisville, Kentucky 40218, is open 11:30 a.m. to 10 p.m. Monday through Thursday, until 11 p.m. Friday and Saturday, with continuous service; dinner menu begins at 4 p.m. Sunday Brunch is from 11 a.m. to 2:30 p.m. (502)456-1111. Dress is casual, although shorts are not allowed; all beverages are sold, and reservations are a good idea on weekends. AE, DC, MC, V. ($$)

JOHN E's POPPY SEED DRESSING

1 ½ cups sugar
2 teaspoons dry mustard
2 teaspoons salt
⅔ cup cider vinegar
4 Tablespoons fresh onion juice

2 cups salad oil (never olive)
3 Tablespoons poppy seed

Mix sugar, mustard, salt, vinegar, and onion juice. Stir well. Beat in oil slowly, and add poppy seeds. Yields 3 cups.

JOHN E's SPLIT PEA SOUP

2 ⅛ cups green split peas
Meaty hambone
12 peppercorns
½ cup chopped onions
2 cups chopped celery with leaves

3 cups sliced carrots
1 cup milk
2 cups beef bouillon
6 Kosher-style garlic frankfurters, sliced

In large pot, soak peas in two quarts water overnight. Bring to boil in same water, reduce heat, add hambone and peppercorns, cover and simmer for one hour. Add vegetables and simmer an additional hour. Remove hambone, cut meat from it, discard bone and chop meat fine. Press soup through food mill; add chopped ham, milk, bouillon, and frankfurters and simmer 20 minutes. Add salt if necessary. Serves ten.

JOHN E's QUICHE LORRAINE

One 9-inch baked pie shell
1 slice bacon, cooked crisp
and chopped
4 thin slices onion, sautéed
1 ½ ounces ham, shredded
1 ½ ounces Swiss cheese,
grated
1 Tablespoon sliced
mushrooms

4 ounces cream
2 eggs
⅛ teaspoon salt
⅛ teaspoon pepper
½ teaspoon hot sauce
¼ clove garlic, minced

Sprinkle bacon, onions, half of ham and half of cheese in pie shell; follow with rest of ham and rest of cheese, then mushrooms. Heat cream in saucepan. In mixing bowl, combine eggs, salt and pepper, hot sauce, and garlic, whip until frothy, and add hot cream, continuing to whip. Pour this mixture into pie shell, and bake at 325 degrees for 25-30 minutes or until top is golden brown. Serves eight.

JOHN E's PECAN PIE

One 9-inch unbaked pie
shell
4 large eggs
1 ⅛ cup light brown sugar,
packed

¼ cup butter, melted
1 cup white corn syrup
¼ teaspoon salt
1 teaspoon vanilla
2 ounces broken pecans

Mix eggs, sugar, butter, syrup, salt and vanilla until well blended but not foamy. Pour into pie shell and sprinkle with pecans. Cook at 400 degrees for ten minutes, turn oven thermostat to 350 degrees, and open oven door for 15 minutes. Close oven door and continue to bake until just set. Serves eight.

BAUER'S since 1870
Louisville

WHEN THE HIGHWAY

from Louisville to Brownsboro was a toll road, there was a way-station at the tollgate where travelers who were "benighted," or overtaken by darkness on the road, could be guaranteed a safe haven for the night, and perhaps a simple meal. Later, the way-station became a blacksmith shop run by John Bauer, and Mrs. Bauer began a family tradition by serving soups and sandwiches to people waiting for their horses to be shod.

Automobiles put the blacksmith shop out of business in the early 1920's, and Bauer's became a restaurant in earnest. As its popularity grew, the family gave up their quarters one room at a time to increase dining space.

Always a family-operated restaurant, Bauer's is now in its fourth generation, with Charles F. "Skee" Bauer, general manager, and John "Jay" Southard, assistant manager, offering the German foods which have been popular from the beginning, as well as regional favorites. Family members continue working well into their 80's, and many customers have been faithful for more than 50 years—there's a family feeling about Bauer's that expands to include first-time visitors. No reservations are taken, and people of all ages wait cheerfully and companionably for dinner, proving that Bauer's has more to offer than just good food.

Bauer's has been extensively remodeled since a disastrous fire on Easter Sunday, 1984, but the bar, the nucleus of the establishment, still retains its hearty 19th century tavern atmosphere. There are, however, now barstools and tables in what was once a strictly stand-up room.

The main dining room is formal, with a pink marble fireplace, Queen Anne-style armchairs, colorful bird wallpaper, and huge brass chandeliers. The west room, smaller and cozier, has the same color scheme of light wood paneling and deep green carpets; booths are separated by green velvet curtains, and wing chairs at tables are covered in the same fabric. French doors open onto a walled brick patio where meals are served in warm weather.

Bauer's lighter salad-sandwich lunch menu also features the superb soups, Smearcase Cheese, Hot German Slaw, and Kentucky limestone Bibb lettuce salad that are popular in the evenings. Dinner entrées chosen from a wide selection of seafood, chicken, pork, beef, veal, and lamb include potato, vegetable, salad, and fresh baked bread. All foods are painstakingly prepared, thoughtfully served, and are as attractive as they are delicious.

Bauer's since 1870, 3612 Brownsboro Road, Louisville, Kentucky 40207, is open 11 a.m. to 2 a.m. Monday through Saturday, with continuous service. (502)895-5493. There is no dress code, and all beverages are sold. Reservations are taken only for parties of ten or more. AE, CB, DC, MC, V. ($$)

BAUER'S SINCE 1870 STUFFED POTATOES

5 large potatoes, baked	⅓ cup shredded mild
2 Tablespoons finely	Cheddar cheese
chopped cooked bacon	½ cup sour cream
2 Tablespoons finely	4 Tablespoons melted
chopped onion	butter
1 Tablespoon grated	⅓ cup milk
Parmesan cheese	½ teaspoon white pepper
1 Tablespoon dried chives	1 teaspoon seasoning salt

Cut potatoes in half lengthwise; scoop potato out and reserve shells. Mix potato with remaining ingredients. Using pastry bag or spoon, mound mixture in six potato shells. Cover and refrigerate or freeze. To serve, thaw completely, brush with melted butter, sprinkle with paprika, and heat slowly at 300 degrees. When hot, lightly brown under broiler and serve. Reserve unfilled shells for potato skins. Serves six

BAUER'S SINCE 1870 BRUDDY CURRAN SANDWICH
(Named for the longtime customer who created it)

2 pieces white toast	6 slices onion
4 pieces cooked bacon	Bacon grease for frying
6 slices tomato	Sliced American cheese

On ovenproof platter, arrange toast and top with bacon. Fry tomato and onion in bacon grease, drain well, and spread on top of bacon. Cover completely with sliced cheese. Bake at 350 degrees until cheese is melted. Serves one.

BAUER'S SINCE 1870 BLUE CHEESE DRESSING

½ pound blue cheese, crumbled

1 Tablespoon distilled white vinegar

1 Tablespoon Worcestershire sauce

1 Tablespoon olive or salad oil

3 ½ cups mayonnaise

¼ cup milk

2 dashes red pepper sauce

Mix all ingredients well; allow to sit overnight before using. Yields about 1 quart.

CUNNINGHAM'S
Louisville

WITH ITS STRONG HERI-

tage of ethnic neighborhoods, Louisville has always had its favorite taverns, where like-minded people could meet for conversation over beer and a sandwich. These friendly gathering places often develop a clientele that continues for generations.

One of Louisville's most enduring is Cunningham's, strategically located near downtown business and fine old residential areas now under restoration. It began in 1870, as a grocery and delicatessen with a livery stable in the rear, and became a preferred lunching place for carters and draymen. By 1890, a beer bar had replaced the grocery, sporting tiled walls and floor, stained glass windows advertising beer, and a huge oak back bar to dominate the room.

The legends of Cunningham's out-distance the facts: it is believed to have harbored at various times a gambling den, people of questionable morals and habits, and an upstairs brothel.

When "Cap" Cunningham became the new owner, the illegal upstairs activities ended, and a respectable, reasonable, and very popular restaurant was developed. During Prohibition, however, a beverage known as "Cap's Soft Drink" failed to meet the standards set by the government, and the restaurant was closed, briefly, only to open to new prosperity at the end of the depression.

As business (of whatever kind) grew, so did the building, expanding to connect the restaurant in the front with the stable at the rear. The stable became a "liquor bar," and private rooms upstairs consumed every cranny.

Cunningham's never again achieved a shady reputation; in 1942 it was Louisville's first drive-in restaurant, and is fondly remembered as THE place to go with a group for recuperation from exams, or to celebrate a birthday. Children love the cubicles and private rooms, and the menu appeals to all ages.

Fried fish is a specialty—Owner Don George says 4,000 pounds of fish are sold each month, with 8,000 pounds of hand-cut french fries. Other items are what George calls "plain old American food," but Cunningham's popularity indicates otherwise. Items in demand are homemade soups—including superb turtle soup and chili—old fashioned corned beef and cabbage, hot roast beef with gravy, seafood, steaks, and country ham.

A full list of sandwiches is topped by the ½ pound Cunningham Burger; vegetables and salads are equally generous, and desserts like walnut or chocolate cake, cheesecake, and lemon, walnut, or cherry pie are just right to end a satisfying eating experience.

Cunningham's, 900 South Fifth Street, Louisville, Kentucky 40203, is open from 11 a.m. to 10 p.m. Monday through Thursday, to 11 p.m. Friday and Saturday, with continuous service. Cafeteria service is available in the front bar from 11 a.m. to 2 p.m. weekdays. (502)587-0526. All beverages are served, dress is casual, and reservations are taken for lunch and evening; all items are available for carryout. AE, DC, MC, V. ($)

CUNNINGHAM'S TURTLE SOUP

1 pound turtle meat
One 15-ounce can whole
  kernel corn
One 6-ounce can tomato
  paste
One 10 ¾-ounce can tomato
  purée
1 teaspoon salt

¼ cup Worcestershire
  sauce
Spice bag of whole allspice
  in cheesecloth bag
5 ½ ounces precooked
  barley
2 cups Burgundy wine

Put turtle meat and corn through coarse blade of grinder. In very large pot, place ground meat mixture with tomato paste and purée, salt, Worcestershire sauce, and spice bag with one gallon of water. Cook slowly for 1 ½ hours.

Add barley and cook for an additional hour. Allow to cool for one hour, add Burgundy, heat through, and serve. Yields about five quarts.

CUNNINGHAM'S SPINACH CASSEROLE

One 15-ounce can spinach
OR
Two 10-ounce packages
frozen chopped spinach
1 egg
½ cup Cheez Whiz

½ cup bread crumbs
2 Tablespoons dried onion
1 Tablespoon butter or
margarine, melted
¼ cup half and half cream
Lemon juice, optional

Drain spinach well, pressing down with back of spoon. Mix all ingredients thoroughly. Pour into buttered casserole and bake at 350 degrees until bubbly.

CUNNINGHAM'S BLEU CHEESE DRESSING

2 cups mayonnaise
Pinch of garlic powder
1 Tablespoon half and half
cream

¼ cup crumbled blue
cheese
1 ounce white wine

Blend all ingredients; store in refrigerator. Yields about a pint.

CUNNINGHAM'S THOUSAND ISLAND DRESSING

2 cups mayonnaise
¼ cup sweet pickle relish

1 ounce tomato catsup

Blend all ingredients; store in refrigerator. Yields about a pint.

SIXTH AVENUE
Louisville

IT WAS BUILT IN THE MID-
1850's, and had served as a business house and a men's and
boy's clothing store; in 1880, Louis Seelbach opened a bar,
restaurant, and billiard room in the building at the corner
of Sixth and Main. By 1886, it was a hotel, and Louis' younger
brother Otto had joined him in a prospering business. Remodeling in 1900 incorporated a stained glass light well, Flemish
oak yoke beams in the lobby, and an elaborate plaster ceiling
and marble floor in the bar.

When the Seelbachs opened their "Grand Hotel" at Fourth
and Walnut in 1905, their original hotel was renamed "The
Old Inn," a colorful place that catered primarily to men. After
a period as a men's dry goods store, the building was a
mailorder showroom from the 1940's until 1976, when it was
boarded up and became a haven for vagrants for three years.

Courageous restoration, at a time when Main Street was not
a fashionable address, won numerous awards for excellence
in adaptive re-use; when the building was completed in 1980,
there was a new restaurant, owned by Louisville's famed
Grisanti family, at the street level. The stained glass was gone,
but the oak beams and plasterwork were uncovered behind
false ceilings, and the bar was returned to its original use. The
light well now lends a glow to dining at award-winning Sixth
Avenue, one of Louisville's most popular restaurants.

Executive Chef Mark describes Sixth Avenue's emphasis
on American Cuisine as "things our grandmothers brought
to this country and adapted to the regions in which they
settled." He likes to search out "foods people eat on their
vacations" and updates them to create such items as Kitty
Hawk Spiced Shrimp, Pan Fried Catfish (in orange butter
with candied orange zest), and "Owensboro" boned, barbecued
chicken, whipped potatoes, roasted beets, and herbed cornbread—help account for the restaurant's many awards.

The freshest and highest quality foods, are presented with
imagination; seafoods are emphasized, as is veal, and there
is always something special in addition to the menu. Tableside
desserts have clever names—try Bananas Stephen Foster
(with bourbon), or Pralines Pauline's.

Sixth Avenue, 600 West Main Street, Louisville, Kentucky 40202, is open for lunch Monday through Saturday from 11:30 a.m. to 2:30 p.m., for dinner Monday through Thursday from 5 to 11 p.m., until 12 midnight on Friday and Saturday. A theatre menu is available from 5 to 7 p.m. Monday through Saturday. (502)587-6664. Coat and tie are suggested for men; all beverages and an extensive wine list are available, with 17 wines sold by the glass; and reservations are recommended, especially from September through June and during productions at the Kentucky Center for the Arts. AE, CB, D, MC, V. ($$$)

SIXTH AVENUE LOBSTER BAR HARBOR

Ten 1-pound lobsters
Olive oil for sautéeing
2 large onions, diced
2 pounds mushrooms,
  sliced
10 ounces pimiento, diced
1 quart white wine

1 gallon shelfish stock
5 ounces tomato paste
1 to 1 ½ pounds roux (equal
  parts butter and flour)
Salt, pepper, and tarragon
1 pint cream
Hollandaise sauce

In large pot, poach lobsters in 3 gallons boiling water 12 to 13 minutes. Shock in ice water to stop cooking.

Cut lobsters from middle to head and split through the eyes—do not cut completely in half. From middle to tail, sever shell and crack to keep tail meat whole. Remove meat and coral and reserve; rinse shells and reserve.

In 2-gallon pot, heat olive oil very hot. Sauté onions until soft; add mushrooms, pimiento, and shallots. Sauté two minutes and add coral; cook five minutes to evaporate ammonia. Add wine and boil until reduced by one third; add stock and tomato paste and simmer about 1 ½ hours.

In bowl, crumble roux and soften with a little stock. Add to stock and simmer 30 minutes. Season to taste; whip in cream and chill.

Toss lobster meat in sauce; stuff shells. Bake at 400 degrees for ten minutes and top with Hollandaise sauce. Serves ten.

SIXTH AVENUE HERBED CORNBREAD

2 cups milk
1 cup cornmeal
2 sticks butter, softened
½ teaspoon salt
1 Tablespoon sugar

1 ounce fine herbs (thyme
  rosemary, oregano)
1 ½ Tablespoons bourbon
5 eggs, separated

Preheat oven to 350 degrees. In a saucepan, scald the milk, stir in cornmeal, beat thoroughly, and cook over low heat until thick.

Remove from heat; add butter, salt, sugar and herbs and beat until butter has melted. Set aside to cool.

Beat yolks and stir into mixture with bourbon.

Beat whites until stiff, and fold into cornmeal mixture. Pour into buttered loaf pan and bake 40 minutes, or until golden brown. Slice and toast; serve cut into triangles.

SIXTH AVENUE AMERICAN WILD BERRIES IN PASTRY WITH MELON SAUCE

2 sheets Pepperidge Farm
  puff pastry, thawed
Beaten egg for egg wash
8 ounces brown sugar
1 pint sour cream
4 ounces Midori melon
  liqueur

1 pint raspberries
1 pint blueberries
1 pint black raspberries
1 pint strawberries
Wild spearmint for garnish

Using a round cookie cutter or stencil about 2 ½" in diameter, trace and cut out ten circles of puff pastry and lay them on a cookie sheet which has been lined with parchment or freezer paper. With a paring knife, trace or score lightly a ¼" border, then score the pastry into diamond shapes. Lightly paint pastry with egg wash and bake at 400 degrees until golden brown. Set aside.

In a mixing bowl, combine brown sugar and sour cream and whip until smooth. Whip in Midori. On each serving plate, ladle 3 ounces of melon sauce until it reaches border of plate. Using a knife, cut around border of pastry rounds and remove inner circle to make a lid.

Wash berries and toss together lightly. Fill pastry rounds with berries. Place one on each plate on pool of sauce and top with more sauce, then place lids on top, slightly offset. Garnish with wild spearmint. Serves ten.

THE SEELBACH HOTEL
Louisville

AFTER 25 YEARS IN THE hotel business, Louis and Otto Seelbach were ready to dazzle the traveling world with a lavish new building at the corner of Fourth and Walnut Streets. The year was 1905, and people of taste pampered themselves with every luxury; the "Grand Hotel" with its spacious lobby and sweeping stairway, was immediately popular.

Designed in Beaux-Arts Baroque, an architectural style incorporating elements of several historic periods, the hotel is impressive in its use of the finest materials and embellishments. The lower two stories are of Bowling Green stone, the eight above of Harvard brick with stone trimming, and the soaring two-story lobby, with its murals and arched skylight of beveled glass, is walled and floored with marble.

Every amenity was made available to patrons: a special reception room for ladies; a rathskeller with vaulted ceiling, finished entirely in Rookwood tile; a magnificent billiard room paneled in mahogany; and a roof garden that could be enclosed in winter.

The heart of downtown Louisville moved south with the Seelbach; Fourth Avenue was an exclusive shopping district, and was used as a promenade by the fashionable for decades. With the decline of downtown (in Louisville and across the nation) The Seelbach fell on hard times, and frantic remodeling in an effort to attract business was often injudicious. Although many of the hotel's glorious features were obscured, they were not destroyed, and it was placed on the National Register in 1975.

Restoration, completed in 1982, exposed lobby murals hidden behind plaster and removed the false ceiling covering the vaulted ceiling and skylight. With the greatest care and attention to detail, The Seelbach was returned to The Age of Elegance.

The Oak Room, the Seelbach's flagship restaurant, utilizes only products indigenous to the continental United States, with fresh produce, baked goods prepared on the premises, and seafood flown in four times daily. Hot and cold appetizers, exquisite soups and salads, and entrées of fish, meat, game, and grilled specialties reflect the best of American contemporary cuisine. A Champagne Bar on the nearby mezzanine offers the finest sparkling wines by the glass.

The Café at the Seelbach is more casual and relaxed, offering homemade soups, creative salads—julienne of turkey, ham, cheese and roast beef on spinach—homemade pastas, such entrées as Frittata with Braised Vegetables and Herbs, and "good honest American food" in the atmosphere of a country-French bistro. Wonderful pastries are available to eat or to carry out.

The Seelbach Hotel, 500 Fourth Avenue, Louisville, Kentucky 40202 (502)585-3200. The Oak Room is open for dinner from 6 to 10 p.m., Monday through Thursday, until 11 p.m. Friday and Saturday, and for Sunday Brunch (seasonal) from 11 a.m. to 3 p.m. Jackets are required for men, and reservations are requested. ($$$) The Café at The Seelbach is open for breakfast, lunch, and dinner, from 6:30 a.m. to 11:30 p.m., seven days a week, with continuous service. Dress is casual, and reservations are not required. ($$) In both dining rooms, in the lounge, and on the mezzanine, all beverages are served. AE, CB, D, MC, V.

THE SEELBACH HOTEL SHRIMP IN CREAM AND GREEN PEPPERCORNS

4 shrimp, peeled and deveined	2 ounces heavy cream
Oil for sautéeing	1 orange, peeled and segmented
1 ounce white wine	3 ounces sliced almonds, toasted
1 ounce Curaçao liqueur	1 ounce parsley, chopped
1 ounce green peppercorns	

Sauté shrimp in hot oil for three minutes, add white wine, Curaçao, and peppercorns. Cook over medium heat for one minute, and add heavy cream. Cook an additional minute, add orange segments. Remove shrimp, arrange on plate in a circle with tails touching. Arrange orange segments between shrimp. Cover with sauce. Garnish with almonds and parsley in center of shrimp. Serves one.

THE SEELBACH HOTEL BEEF MEDALLIONS WITH KENTUCKY HAM AND BLUE CHEESE

Three 2-ounce slices of beef tenderloin
CLARIFIED butter OR oil for sautéeing
3 mushrooms, quartered
2 ounces Kentucky ham, cut in julienne
1 ounce port wine
2 ounces beef gravy
1 ounce blue cheese

In hot skillet, sauté beef in CLARIFIED butter or oil 1½ minutes on each side for medium rare. Remove meat from pan; if oil was used for sautéeing, drain oil. Add mushrooms and ham to pan and sauté 2 or 3 minutes, then add port and cook to reduce liquid. Stir in beef gravy and blue cheese; arrange medallions on plate and top with sauce. Serves one.

THE SEELBACH HOTEL SALMON WITH SHRIMP AND CUCUMBER

One 7-ounce salmon steak
Court bouillon (see below)
2 shrimp
1 ounce cream
1 cup white wine
2 ounces butter
1 ounce fresh dill
Salt and pepper
½ cucumber, peeled and sliced

In saucepan, place salmon and cover with court bouillon. Slowly simmer for six to eight minutes. After five minutes, add shrimp. The salmon is finished when it feels firm. Remove salmon and shrimp and set aside.

In another saucepan, heat cream and simmer 2 minutes. Add white wine and simmer an additional minute. Stir in butter, dill, and salt and pepper to taste.

Pour sauce onto serving plate. Place salmon in middle, and arrange shrimp and cucumber on sides of fish. Serves one.

For court bouillon:
1 cup white vinegar
2 cups white wine
2 bay leaves
2 ounces celery, chopped
2 ounces carrots, chopped
2 ounces onion, chopped
2 cups water
1 teaspoon whole white pepper

In saucepan, mix ingredients. Bring to slow boil for three minutes. Remove from heat, strain, and reserve.

THE BROWN HOTEL
Louisville

IN OCTOBER, 1923, AT THE corner of Fourth and Broadway, the Brown Hotel opened, bringing Louisville into big-city status. The brick and stone edifice connected the downtown business district with residential areas south of Broadway, spurring continuing growth of an already thriving downtown.

Within five years, theatres and professional office buildings were grouped around The Brown, a personal expression of its owner, James Graham Brown. The Louisville businessman and philanthropist lived in the penthouse, keeping a watchful eye on everything in the hotel.

During its years as a hotel The Brown welcomed celebrities and soldiers, dancers and debutantes, horse trainers and little ladies in white gloves. In the 1937 flood, with three feet of water in the lobby, it housed a thousand homeless people, while the radio station on the 15th floor broadcast news and hope 24 hours a day.

Suburban growth caused its decline and demise, and it closed in February, 1971. The building was used briefly by the Jefferson County Board of Education and was placed on the National Register in 1978, but then stood vacant.

Downtown redevelopment worked its way up Fourth Street, now closed to traffic, and The Broadway Project Corporation, a non-profit organization, was formed in 1980 to improve the Broadway end of Fourth Street. The award-winning restoration of The Brown Hotel was part of an ambitious plan to restore a 3-block, 33 acre area. Theatre Square, adjacent to the hotel, is underway, with residential communities, offices, and retail space yet to come.

At the NEW Brown, opened in January, 1985, fine food is again served in the beautifully paneled English Grill. Sunday brunch is available in the restored Bluegrass Room, and a new restaurant, J. Graham's Café, offers a more casual atmosphere and lighter food.

And the Hot Brown Sandwich, a Kentucky institution that has been imitated and adapted by nearly every restaurant in the state, is once more available in the place of its origin.

In addition to the Hot Brown (which constitutes 50% of lunch orders), lunch in The English Grill features soups and salads—the Kentucky Bibb Lettuce with Bay Shrimp and Far East Dressing is extraordinary—sandwiches, omelets, and entrées such as Beef and Kidney Pot Pie. The dinner menu is Continental, with hot and cold appetizers, special salads, and entrées of perhaps veal or duck or game combinations with brandied juniper berry sauce. Desserts for both meals, chosen from a cart, are elegant and delicious.

J. Graham's Café, bright and open and overlooking the passing crowd on Fourth Avenue, has a selection of interesting appetizers, salads, and sandwiches, with a daily soup/salad special and, at dinner, some appetizers in entrée portions. Complimentary hors d'oeuvre are available from 4 to 7 p.m.

The Brown Hotel, Fourth and Broadway, Louisville, Kentucky 40202 (502)583-1234. The English Grill is open 11:30 a.m. to 3 p.m. Monday through Saturday for lunch, 5:30 to 11 p.m. Monday through Sunday for dinner. Jackets are preferred for men, and jeans are not allowed; reservations are suggested. ($$$) J.Graham's Café is open from 6:30 a.m. to 11 p.m. seven days a week, with continuous service. Dress is casual, and reservations are not taken. ($) The Bluegrass Room is open only for Sunday Brunch, from 11 a.m. to 3 p.m., and reservations are suggested. In all dining rooms, all beverages are served, with a large selection of non-alcoholic and low-alcohol cocktails as well. AE, CB, Hilton, MC, V.

THE HOT BROWN SANDWICH

2 pieces toasted bread, crusts removed, cut in half
4 ounces sliced white turkey meat

Hot Brown sauce (see below)
Parmesan cheese
2 slices cooked bacon
2 tomato wedges

On very hot oven-proof plate, place bread, top with hot turkey, and pour over Hot Brown sauce. Sprinkle with Parmesan, broil until golden brown, criss-cross with bacon, and garnish with tomato wedges. Serves one.

Hot Brown sauce:
2 cups Bechamel sauce (see below)
½ cup sherry

½ cup Romano Cheese, freshly grated
2 egg yolks, beaten

Into hot prepared Bechamel, beat sherry (boiled until alcohol is cooked out), cheese, and yolks. Stir until blended.

Bechamel sauce:

2 cups milk	About 4 Tablespoons
½ cup heavy cream	butter
1 onion, chopped fine	About 4 Tablespoons flour
1 clove, crushed	

In saucepan, bring milk and cream to boil with onion and clove. Thicken with butter and flour rubbed together to a paste. Cook until flour taste is gone.

THE BROWN HOTEL'S ESCARGOT
CHABLISIENNE
(from The English Grill)

6 escargots	3 inches of garlic butter log
Butter for sautéeing	(see below)
White wine	
6 teaspoons duxelles (see below)	

In small pan, sauté escargots briefly in butter and wine.

In escargot dish, place one teaspoon duxelles in each of six depressions. Top with one escargot on top, then ½-inch piece of garlic butter log. Bake at 350 degrees until butter bubbles, and serve immediately. Serves one.

For duxelles:

2 sausage links, paper removed	1 cup finely chopped mushrooms
½ teaspoon garlic	Salt and pepper to taste

Sauté all ingredients together until moisture is gone.

For garlic butter:

1 pound unsalted butter, softened	½ teaspoon minced garlic
1 teaspoon finely chopped parsley	2 dashes Worcestershire sauce
	1 splash white wine

Fold together, form the mixture into a log and chill.

OLD TALBOTT TAVERN
Bardstown

TO THE FRONTIER TRAV-
eler, making his lonely way through the wilderness, the lights
of a crossroads tavern were a welcome sight. Here he would
find warmth, food, companionship, stabling for his horse, and
a safe haven for the night. There would be news of the civilized
world and the new country to the west, and perhaps even a
precious newspaper.

Many taverns were little more than hospitable homes; others were authorized to "provide in said ordinary good whole-
some food and lodging and drink for travelers," as stated in
the 1785 tavern license, signed by Patrick Henry, which may
be seen at Old Talbott Tavern.

Constructed at the intersection of important north-south
and east-west trails in 1779, Old Talbott Tavern is believed
to be the oldest continuously operating tavern in the country.
It was placed on the National Register of Historic Places in
1973.

The original portion of the tavern, with stone walls two
feet thick, faced east; a public room and kitchen were downstairs, and the upstairs was divided into quarters for men
and women. Traces of the staircase may be seen in the tap-
room ceiling, where smoke-stained beams attest to two hundred years of use.

Visitors may lunch in this room, which served General
George Rogers Clark as headquarters during the Revolution.
Among other famous guests were Henry Clay, Andrew Jackson, William Henry Harrison, and Aaron Burr. Young Abraham Lincoln and his family stayed in the upstairs front room
during a trial for ownership of the family farm; they lost,
and moved to Indiana. Lodging is still available in that room
and five others, each with its own interesting history and
modern comforts.

Old Talbott Tavern has had a number of structural additions; a brick building similar to the original tavern was constructed parallel to it, and the courtyard between the two
was enclosed to form the present lobby. Diners will enjoy
the early 1800's Colonial Room, in which Queen Marie of
Roumania had tea in 1926, and the upstairs room where,

according to tradition, murals painted by companions of exiled King Louis Phillippe were defaced by Jesse James, who fired his pistols at the pictures.

Under the direction of General Manager Bill Kelley, whose father, John S. Kelley, is proprietor, Old Talbott Tavern's foods reflect current tastes, with a traditional flavor. Luncheon soups and salads are joined on the menu by country ham, beef, and seafood entrées; dinners feature Southern fried chicken, fried country ham, quail, and two chicken-ham combinations. Homemade breads and a very special chess pie top off a generous meal.

Old Talbott Tavern, 107 W. Stephen Foster, Bardstown, Kentucky 40004, is open for lunch from 11 a.m. to 3 p.m., and for dinner from 5 to 9 p.m., seven days a week. Lighter fare is available from 3 to 5 p.m. and until 10 p.m. on Saturdays. (502)348-3494. Bardstown is two miles off the Bluegrass Parkway, about 50 miles southwest of Lexington. Dress is casual, all beverages are available, and reservations are requested for a party of six or more or for overnight guests. AE, DC, MC, V. ($$)

TALBOTT TAVERN GOURMET

1 slice country ham, fried
About ½ cup wild rice, cooked
½ chicken breast, boned
Flour for dredging, seasoned with salt and pepper
Lard for frying
Worcestershire sauce
Poultry seasoning
Bay leaf
2 to 3 teaspoons red wine vinegar
1 Tablespoon brandy
1 to 2 Tablespoons Burgundy wine

Dredge chicken breast in seasoned flour; in skillet, braise in lard until flour is browned. Place in oven-proof pan, season with Worcestershire sauce, poultry seasoning, and top with bay leaf and wine vinegar. Cover and bake at 350 degrees 20 minutes or until done. During the last five minutes, uncover, remove from oven, and flame with brandy. Replace in oven when flame is out. Just before serving, ladle Burgundy on top. Serve on fried country ham with wild rice. Serves one.

OLD TALBOTT TAVERN CORN FRITTERS

2 cups self rising flour
¼ teaspoon sugar
1 egg

¼ cup whole kernel corn,
   drained
Milk

Mix all ingredients, using just enough milk to moisten; batter should be stiff. Drop by tablespoon into deep oil at 325 degrees and fry to a golden brown. Roll in powdered sugar and serve warm.

OLD TALBOTT TAVERN SAUSAGE SOUFFLÉ

½ pound hot sausage
½ pound mild sausage
12 slices white bread,
   buttered
2 cups grated sharp cheese

8 eggs
Worcestershire sauce
4 cups milk
1 teaspoon salt
1 teaspoon dry mustard

Crumble, cook, and drain sausage. Trim and cube bread. Butter a 3-quart casserole and line with half the bread. Sprinkle with one cup cheese, add sausage, and top with rest of bread and cheese. Beat eggs with milk and seasonings, pour over casserole, and refrigerate overnight. Bring casserole to room temperature; bake at 325 degrees 45 minutes to an hour. Serves 10 to 12.

OLD TALBOTT TAVERN PIE

One 9-inch baked pie shell
¾ cup sugar
½ cup flour
¼ teaspoon salt
2 egg yolks, beaten

½ cup orange juice
1 Tablespoon grated
   orange rind
2 Tablespoons lemon juice
Whipped cream for garnish

Combine sugar, flour, and salt in top of double boiler, add 1 ¼ cups water, and stir until smooth. Cook and stir over direct heat for 5 minutes. Remove from heat, add yolks and cook 5 minutes longer over boiling water, stirring constantly. Remove from heat and add fruit juices and rind. Chill and turn into pie shell. To serve, top with whipped cream. Serves eight.

LA TABERNA
Bardstown

St. Joseph's Proto-Cathedral

St. JOSEPH'S PROTO-CAthedral, the first Roman Catholic cathedral west of the Alleghenies, was once the seat of a diocese that included the entire Northwest Territory. The cathedral, now designated a National Landmark, was completed in 1819, and that same year, St. Joseph's Southern Catholic College was established. Although the original college building was destroyed by fire in 1838, it was replaced almost immediately.

The new structure, named for Father Martin Spalding, was the main building of the college, first under parish priests, and after 1848, under the Jesuits. The school was closed during the War Between the States, but Spalding Hall was used as a hospital by both Union and Confederate forces.

After the war the school reopened as a seminary, and in the ensuing years it was again a college, an orphanage, and last a preparatory school, closing in 1968. Spalding Hall stood empty and badly in need of repair for two years; it had been offered for community use when Neal and Mickie Clark decided to renovate the basement for a restaurant.

After six months of strenuous cleaning, followed by sandblasting, the original brick arches without keystones were visible. The beautifully vaulted ceilings of what had been the boys' locker rooms and laundry became an unusual restaurant with a "wine cellar" feeling, with exposed rose-colored brick walls and a floor of solid bedrock. It was named "La Taberna" for an arched tavern in ancient Greece, and opened in 1971.

Renovation of the entire building followed, and resulted in multiple occupancy; placed on the National Register in 1973, Spalding Hall also houses an art gallery, The Bardstown Historical Museum, and the Oscar Getz Museum of Whiskey History.

La Taberna is not the easiest of these to locate; the entrance is on the side of the building, through wrought-iron gates and a long corridor, but it is worth the effort. Don't miss a peek at the banquet hall in the former chapel!

Guests begin each meal at the Appetizer Bar, with oysters on the half shell, a special soup (often onion) with homemade garlic toast, fried mushrooms, cauliflower, and a unique vegetable stick. Entrées are regional: baked or fried Kentucky ham, prime rib, chicken livers; or Continental: Veal Scallopine, Chicken Kiev or Cordon Bleu; and fresh seafood as available. All vegetables are freshly prepared, with several popular vegetable casseroles. Salad dressings and breads are homemade, as are fruit cobblers, pies, strawberry shortcake, and plain or chocolate chip cheesecake.

La Taberna, 112 N. 5th Street at Xavier Drive, Bardstown, Kentucky 40004, is open for dinner only, Monday through Saturday from 5 to 10 p.m.; the lounge is open until 12 midnight, and until 1 a.m. during the summer. Luncheons for groups are by reservation only. (502)348-3946. Dress is informal, all beverages are served, and reservations are necessary only for large groups. AE, DC, MC, V. ($$)

LA TABERNA CHICKEN CORDON BLEU

1 chicken breast, boned	Flour for dredging
Salt and pepper	1 egg, beaten
1 slice ham	Bread or cracker crumbs
1 slice Swiss cheese	Oil for sautéeing

Flatten chicken breast by pounding with cleaver on the inside. Season with salt and pepper; place ham and cheese on one side. Fold and dredge in flour, dip in egg, then in crumbs.

In skillet, sauté until brown. Place on sheet pan, and bake at 350 degrees until done. Serves one.

LA TABERNA LAMB FRIES

"Lamb Fries" is the local euphemism for the testes of young sheep, a delicacy of long tradition in Kentucky.

Lamb fries	Cracker meal
1 egg, beaten	Deep fat for frying
1 cup milk	

Slice lamb fries ¼ inch thick; slicing will be easier if they are partially frozen. Combine egg and milk; dip lamb fry slices in this batter, then roll in cracker meal. Fry in deep fat at 300 degrees until golden brown.

LA TABERNA KENTUCKY PIE

One 9-inch unbaked pie
    shell
½ cup margarine, melted
1 cup sugar
½ cup flour

2 eggs, slightly beaten
1 teaspoon vanilla
¾ cup English walnuts
½ cup chocolate chips

In mixing bowl, mix margarine with sugar and flour; beat in eggs. Add vanilla, then walnuts and chocolate chips. Pour mixture into pie shell, and bake at 350 degrees for 30 minutes. Serves eight.

THE OLD STABLE
Bardstown

NELSON COUNTY, THE

fourth Kentucky county, was established by the Virginia Assembly in 1784, and was named for former Governor Thomas Nelson of Virginia, a signer of the Declaration of Independence, who paupered himself to defend this country.

The county seat was called "Bairdstown" for David Baird, one of the original land owners; the name was later corrupted to Bardstown. In an earlier town on the site called Salem, residents did not hold clear title to the land and in 1788, 130 half-acre lots were laid out and sold by lottery.

According to tradition, Lot 81, near the center of town, has a long history of involvement with transportation. About 1820, it was divided into two parts, the eastern half being used by a blacksmith; a coachmaker occupied the western half. The coach factory became a livery stable in the mid-nineteenth century, and although it burned in 1895, it was rebuilt in the same location, only to become a garage with the coming of the automobile age. Fifty years later, a large building to house trucking equipment was constructed on the rear of the lot, connecting with the old stable.

Its previous usage virtually eradicated, the building became The Old Stable Restaurant in 1975, carrying on the theme of transportation by entertaining hundreds of motor coach tours.

The structure is divided into an elegant room on the left and a rustic tavern on the right. The enormous room at the rear is the site of the all-you-can-eat "Southern Evening Buffet," with four meat entrées (always including top round of beef and smoked ham) eight or ten southern vegetables, salad, and old fashioned fruit cobblers. Relaxed dinner music by the Mountain Dew Hillbillies culminates in an after-dinner sing-a-long and talent show with guest participation.

Those who prefer a quieter meal may be seated in one of the other rooms to order from a menu that owner Steve Hayden describes as "Southern food with a Continental flair." Frontier-flavored country ham, fried chicken, and pork chops are joined by steaks ordered by weight, seafood, and "Country Combinations" from surf and turf.

Sixty per cent of the world's bourbon whiskey is made in

Nelson County, a fact reflected in The Old Stable's "Premium Well," indicating first quality spirits used in all drinks. Over 143 imported beers are stocked, and Kentucky mint juleps are served in official Kentucky Derby souvenir glasses.

The Old Stable, 116 West Stephen Foster Avenue, Bardstown, Kentucky 40004, is open for dinner only, from 4 p.m. to 8:30 p.m. in winter, to 10 p.m. in summer, and is closed on Sundays in winter. (502)348-3040. Breakfast and lunch are served only to groups, by prior arrangement. Dress is "casual to dress up," all beverages are served, and reservations are not required but are advisable. MC, V, First Card Plus. ($$)

OLD STABLE CORN PUDDING

1 Tablespoon flour	Dash of salt
1 Tablespoon sugar	2 cups corn
2 eggs, beaten	2 Tablespoons melted
1 cup milk	butter

Mix together flour and sugar and add to beaten eggs. Add milk and salt and beat. Pour into greased 1 ½ quart casserole, add corn and melted butter. Bake at 400 degrees for 30 minutes, or until golden brown.

OLD STABLE SEASONED GREEN BEANS

1 gallon young, tender green beans	1 teaspoon sugar
Salt pork	Ground red pepper

Snap, break, and wash beans. In large pot, place beans, cover with water, and add several pieces salt pork, sugar, and a sprinkle of red pepper. Cover and simmer for about three hours. Remove cover and boil quickly until liquid is gone. Remove pork and serve hot with buttered corn bread.

OLD STABLE OLD FASHIONED BEAN SOUP

2 pounds dried beans, pinto or Great Northern variety	1 large ham hock

Wash beans, place in a dutch oven, and cover with water. Soak overnight. Pour off water and cover with fresh water, adding the ham hock. Cover and simmer, adding water if necessary, all day. Remove ham hock and serve with corn sticks.

OLD STABLE CORNBREAD STUFFING

4 cups bread crumbs
4 cups cornbread crumbs
½ cup chopped onion
½ cup chopped celery
1 teaspoon sage

3 cups hot turkey broth
⅓ cup melted butter
1 cup milk
Salt and pepper to taste

Combine all ingredients and stuff turkey, or bake in separate dish until brown on top.

DOE RUN INN
Brandenburg

$\mathbf{T}$HE THREE-STORY BUILD-
ing that is now part of Doe Run Inn was built about 1791
on land discovered by Squire Boone, Daniel's preacher
brother, only a few miles from the Ohio River. One of the
first mills in Kentucky, it was an enormous structure for
the time, with a full attic and basement, and fieldstone walls
two and a half feet thick.

Serving at various times as a woolen mill, a "corncracker"
mill, and a flour mill, it was powered by an undershot wheel
turned by water from Doe Run Creek. A two-story section
was added to the main building about 1821, and the mill
continued in operation until 1900.

During pioneer days, mills were among the first signs of
stability in a new settlement; there was a mill on nearly every
little stream, where huge water wheels powered grindstones
that turned the farmer's wheat and corn into dietary staples.
For settlers who seldom ventured far from home, a trip to
a mill was an event long anticipated, and those waiting their
turn had a rare chance to gossip.

Many mills burned, due to the ever-present dry dust and
oil dripped by machinery; others were abandoned or closed
when more modern equipment became readily available. Today the only traces left of some mills are the names of the
country roads that once led to them, and the few that remain
have been electrified or remodeled for other use.

Doe Run Inn became a summer resort around the turn
of this century, and in 1927, when heat and running water
were added, it was converted to year-round use, with 12 overnight lodging rooms and bountiful meals served three times
daily.

Portions of the millrace, stone walls rising three feet above
ground level, may still be seen, but the millwheel is long
gone; the stream flowing past the summer dining porch is
stocked with trout, and wild ducks paddle slowly on its placid
surface.

Visitors enjoy the peaceful surroundings, of 1,000 wooded
acres; five generations of the same family have made this
remote spot known for its restfulness and rustic charm. The

Doe Run Creek Historic District is on the National Register of Historic Places.

Southern fried chicken, country ham, steaks and Kentucky trout are important items on the Doe Run Inn menu, filled out by seafood, salads and sandwiches, and an old-fashioned breakfast each morning. Homemade biscuits and pies are outstanding, and the Friday evening and Sunday noon Smorgasboards offer 80 different items, both hot and cold, for unlimited feasting.

Doe Run Inn, Brandenburg, Kentucky 40108, is four miles south of Brandenburg on KY 448, between U.S. 60 and Route 1638. Breakfast is served 7:30 to 10 a.m., lunch 11:30 a.m. to 3:30 p.m., and dinner 4 to 9 p.m., seven days a week, except Smorgasboard on Friday 5:30 to 9 p.m. and on Sunday 12 noon to 9 p.m. (502)422-2982 or (502)422-2042. The easiest route is I-64 west from Louisville to Corydon, Indiana, and IN 135 south to Brandenburg, about a 30-mile trip. Dress is casual, beer is served, and reservations are necessary for overnight rooms and appreciated for meals for eight or more. V, MC. ($$)

DOE RUN INN THREE BEAN SALAD

One 15 ½-ounce can cut
  green beans
One 15 ½-ounce can wax
  beans
One 15 ½-ounce can dark
  red kidney beans

5 ounces white vinegar
¾ cup granulated sugar
½ cup salad oil
2 Tablespoons chopped
  onion

Drain beans; mix with other ingredients. May be stored in refrigerator up to two weeks. Serves 15.

DOE RUN INN SAUERKRAUT SALAD

16 ounces chopped or
  shredded kraut, drained
½ cup sugar
¼ cup vegetable oil
¼ cup white vinegar

2 Tablespoons chopped
  green pepper
2 Tablespoons chopped
  pimiento

Mix all ingredients. May be stored in refrigerator up to two weeks. Serves six.

DOE RUN INN SOUTHERN FRIED CHICKEN

One 2-½ pound fryer
  chicken, cut into 8 pieces
2 teaspoons salt

1 ½ cups lard or salad oil
2 cups coarse-ground self-
  rising flour

Place chicken pieces in large bowl; cover with cold water, add salt, and soak 30 minutes. In a cast iron skillet, heat 1 ½ inches lard or oil to 370 degrees on a deep-fat thermometer. Roll wet chicken pieces in the flour; for very crusty chicken, dip in water again and roll in flour a second time.

Fry chicken uncovered (if you have no thermometer, fat should bubble when chicken is placed in skillet) for 15 minutes, or until it has a golden crust, then turn pieces and fry another 10 minutes. Drain on paper towels. Serves four.

DOE RUN INN PUMPKIN PIE

Two 9-inch unbaked pie
  shells
3 eggs, separated
½ cup sugar
1 cup light brown sugar
2 Tablespoons flour

1 teaspoon cinnamon
½ teaspoon salt
½ teaspoon nutmeg
1 ¼ cups cooked pumpkin
2 cups milk

Preheat oven to 450 degrees. Set aside egg whites. In a large saucepan, mix well beaten yolks with the rest of the ingredients and cook over medium heat until thickened. Beat egg whites until stiff but not dry, and fold into hot mixture a little at a time. Pour into pie shells, and bake 15 minutes at 450 degrees; reduce heat to 300 degrees, and bake an additional 30 minutes, or until firm. Makes two pies; serves 16.

THE WHISTLE STOP RESTAURANT
Glendale

I**N THE QUAINT COUNTRY**
village of Glendale, time has stood still for generations. White houses starched with gingerbread sprawl in shady yards, neighbors wave as they go about their business, and the only disturbers of the peace are passing trains.

The station is gone now; trains are fewer and no longer stop, but the track still runs through the center of town, and the flavor of the railroad years has been preserved in The Whistle Stop restaurant.

In 1974, James and Idell Sego rebuilt part of his trackside hardware store into a restaurant, incorporating ticket windows and other train station elements. A tumble-down log cabin was brought into town and rebuilt next to the restaurant as a cozy waiting room with a gift shop in the loft.

Soon visitors came from nearby Elizabethtown, and as the word spread, travelers drove the two miles from I-65 for lunch, and groups planned day trips from Louisville and Bowling Green. Gift and antique shops moved into other old buildings, and Glendale became the place to go for an outing and a great meal.

Expansion of The Whistle Stop eventually absorbed the entire hardware store, with new dining areas made to look like separate small buildings within the large one. One room, long and narrow as a train dining car, has wooden booths on each side; another has a gabled roof overhead, while a third is a country kitchen, complete with dry sink and pump, wood stove, and hanging cupboards cluttered with useful vintage implements.

Country antiques are everywhere, and even the necessary facilities are made to look outdoors-y, with painted ivy twining over the door—and even inside.

All the country charm isn't in the decor, however. Idell believes in quality food from the start, prepared with her individual touches. "It's just my own style of home cooking," she said. "Just as at home, I come up with new ideas."

Her lunch ideas might include changing "Trainman Specials" of creamed chicken on cornbread or baked pork chops with potatoes and cream sauce; tasty chicken salad with fruit salad and muffin; or a luncheon steak with potato, salad, and puffy homemade rolls. Dinner specials might be panfried trout, salmon croquettes or stuffed pork chops, served with fresh country vegetables, salad, and homemade bread. Then regular items: homemade soups, sandwiches and burgers, entrees like baked or fried country ham, prime rib, and seafood.

The Whistle Stop's homemade desserts: Sugar Cream Pie (meltingly sweet, with cinnamon) chocolate, coconut and other pies and fruit cobblers have flaky light crusts; if you call ahead, you can take one home. Better yet, take two!

The Whistle Stop Restaurant, Main Street, Glendale, Kentucky 42740, is open 11 a.m. to 9 p.m. Tuesday through Saturday, with a limited menu available from 2 to 5 p.m. (502)369-8586. Dress is casual, and no reservations or credit cards are accepted; personal checks accepted. ($$)

Glendale dates to keep in mind: Glendale Crossing Festival, 3rd Saturday in October; Christmas in the Country, 1st Saturday after December 1; and Derby Brunch at The Whistle Stop, 10 a.m. to 1 p.m., 1st Saturday in May.

WHISTLE STOP KENTUCKY BIBB LETTUCE WITH HOT BACON DRESSING

Medium bowl of Bibb or leaf lettuce

3 or 4 fresh green onions with tops, chopped

4 Tablespoons bacon drippings

2 Tablespoons white vinegar

1 teaspoon sugar

Salt and pepper

4 slices crisp bacon, crumbled

Wash and drain lettuce and tear into bite-sized pieces. Place in bowl and toss with onions. Set aside.

In iron skillet, heat bacon drippings, vinegar, sugar, salt and pepper just to boiling. Pour over lettuce, and toss lightly. Top with crumbled bacon. Serves four to six.

WHISTLE STOP HAM AND ASPARAGUS ROLLS

Fresh asparagus spears, cooked

Margarine or butter, melted

Salt

Nutmeg

Center-cut slices of baked country ham

Hollandaise or mild cheese sauce

Fresh pineapple wedges

152

Toss asparagus spears with small amount of margarine or butter; sprinkle with salt and nutmeg to taste.

Place two asparagus spears on each ham slice and roll up. Top with sauce, garnish with pineapple, and serve.

WHISTLE STOP MOTHER'S SWEET MUFFINS

2 cups all-purpose flour
2 teaspoons baking powder
1 teaspoon salt
¼ cup sugar
⅓ cup oil or melted margarine
1 cup milk

Sift dry ingredients together. Mix oil or margarine with milk, add to dry ingredients quickly and spoon into greased muffin pans. Bake at 425 degrees about 20 minutes, or until brown. Yields 12 large muffins.

WHISTLE STOP FRESH STRAWBERRY TARTS

Six 3-inch baked tart shells
Fresh strawberries
1 cup sugar
3 Tablespoons cornstarch
3 Tablespoons white corn syrup
1 cup cold water
3 Tablespoons strawberry gelatin
Red food coloring
Whipped cream and Fresh mint for garnish

In saucepan, mix sugar and cornstarch. Add syrup and water, bring to a boil, and cook for 2 to 2 ½ minutes over medium heat. Remove from heat, add gelatin and food coloring to desired color, and stir until gelatin is dissolved. Set aside.

Wash and cap berries. Fill tart shells with berries and pour glaze over berries. Refrigerate until glaze has set. Top with whipped cream and a sprig of fresh mint. Serves six.

PATTI'S
of Glasgow

PIONEERS WHO CAME TO
the large open grasslands in south-central Kentucky called
them "Barrens," believing trees would not grow in the area.
Possibly Indians had burned parts of the forest to drive out
game, for trees are abundant now, making this rolling terrain
one of the most attractive parts of Kentucky, with caves and
lakes for drama.

Early exploration was by a band of hunters, who discovered
a large beaver dam and stayed to trap and hunt. Called "Long
Hunters" for the length of time they were away from home,
forty men camped on Beaver Creek during the winter of 1769-
70.

The area was filled with danger from Indians and wild
animals, and remained unsettled until John Hall, a hero of
the Revolutionary War, built a fort beside one of the buffalo
roads that animals carved through the wilderness on their
way to salt licks. A surveyor, he is believed to have been
one of only three residents when Barren County was established in 1798.

Feet of men followed those of buffalo down Salt Works Road,
and John Hall prospered; he built a large house near a spring
on his 1,000 acre military grant, served as one of the county's
first judges, and in the Legislature. Although his home burned
shortly after his death, the beautiful farm remains. A former
tenant house has been converted to a delightful country restaurant overlooking 300 acres of prairie.

Acquired in 1984 by the Tullar Family, Patti's of Glasgow
joins Patti's 1880's (in Grand Rivers) and Patti's on the Pier
(on Green Turtle Bay, Lake Barkley) in an unusual family
operation. The restaurants differ greatly in appearance and
atmosphere, and each is run by a different member of the
family, but are all noted for serving what "Chip" Tullar, in
charge of the Glasgow operation, terms "good, simple, middle-
America cooking. You come here to eat old-fashioned food—
I cook like 30 years ago, like my mother (the famous Patti)
and grandmother."

In a pastel country-French ambience of great charm, Chip
and General Manager Jimma Grimm dispense that "old-fashioned" food with a flair. Hot homemade bread, cooked in a

clay flower pot and served with strawberry butter, accompanies Char-broiled Catfish Filets with butter and rosemary, the grilled 2-inch thick pork chop, steaks or chicken. Lighter entrées and a selection of sandwiches are tempting, but Patti's mile-high meringue pies and other homemade desserts are irresistible.

Try Bill's Boatsinker Pie (gooey fudge in a crust with coffee ice cream, whipped cream, chocolate sauce) Upside-down Strawberry Meringue Pie, or rich caramel-nut John Y. Brown Pie. And you'll find Patti's Boo-Boo Pie is not a mistake at all!

Patti's of Glasgow, Box 295 A, Glasgow, Kentucky 42141, is open Tuesday through Saturday from 11 a.m. to 2 p.m. for lunch, from 5 to 8:30 or 9 p.m. for dinner, and 11:30 a.m. to 2 p.m. for Sunday Brunch. (502)678-1737. It is 2 miles from Glasgow, 14 miles from Mammoth Cave, and about 7 miles from I-65 at the Cave City exit. Dress is casual, reservations are suggested, and there are special prices for children. Setups and glasses are provided for those who bring beverages. AE, MC, V, personal checks. ($$)

PATTI'S STRAWBERRY BUTTER

¾ pound margarine or
butter
16 ounces frozen
strawberries, thawed

½ cup powdered sugar

Bring margarine or butter to room temperature. In mixer bowl, whip butter, strawberries with juice, and sugar. Fresh strawberries may be used in season, adapting sugar to taste.

PATTI'S SHRIMP-SCALLOP BERNICE

1 dozen jumbo shrimp
½ pound butter
½ teaspoon garlic powder
Pinch of sweet basil
Pinch of red pepper
Pinch of curry powder
Pinch of garlic salt

Pinch of seasoned salt
Pinch of minced onion
1 dozen scallops
1 cup white wine
Juice of two lemon wedges
Cornstarch
White or wild rice, cooked

Shell shrimp and cut butterfly style; make a hole in back of each shrimp and pull tail through to make a flower shape. Set aside.

In large skillet, melt butter and add spices and seasonings. Add shrimp and scallops to mixture and cook about 2 minutes, or until seafood is firm. Add wine and simmer two minutes; do not overcook. With slotted spoon, remove seafood and set aside. Add lemon juice to mixture, and thicken with a little cornstarch mixed with water.

Return seafood to mixture, heat through, and serve on rice. Serves four.

PATTI'S DERBY DAY GRITS

2 ½ teaspoons salt
1 ½ cups quick grits
½ cup butter
Two 6-ounce rolls garlic
  cheese spread

Cayenne pepper
3 eggs, separated
Paprika cheese spread

In large pan, combine 6 cups water and salt and bring to a boil. Gradually add grits, and cook over low heat until thickened. Remove from heat, stir in butter, cheese, and cayenne. Stir in lightly beaten yolks. Beat whites stiff and fold into mixture. Pour into greased casserole dish, sprinkle with paprika, and bake at 350 degrees for 45 minutes to one hour or until firm. Serves six.

PATTI'S JOHN Y. BROWN PIE
Named for the former Governor of Kentucky

One 9-inch unbaked pie
  shell
1 cup sugar
½ cup flour
½ cup butter, melted

2 eggs, slightly beaten
6 ounces butterscotch
  chips
1 cup pecan pieces
1 teaspoon vanilla

Mix sugar and flour together; add melted butter and blend well. Stir in eggs, chips, nuts and vanilla, and pour into pie shell. Bake at 325 degrees for one hour or until golden brown. Pie will wiggle when done and set as it cools. Serves eight.

MARIAH'S 1818
Bowling Green

As EARLY AS 1775, HUNT-
ers explored an area near where the Cumberland Trace
crossed the Barren River; McFadden's Station, built at the
crossing about 1785, was an early fort and landmark for travelers. Robert Moore established himself at a nearby "big
spring" in 1790, and in 1797 offered two acres for the construction of public buildings in new Warren County, named for
General Joseph Warren, who fought at Bunker Hill.

Tradition says that court was held at the home of Robert
and his brother George Moore until the construction of a
courthouse, and that visitors often played a game of bowls
on the lawn, giving the new town the name of Bowling Green.

George Moore and his wife Elizabeth built a Federal-style
house at 801 State Street in 1818, at a cost of $4,000. It is
believed to stand on the site of the Moore brothers' original
home, and to be the oldest brick house in Bowling Green.
George Moore died in 1819, but the house continued to be
occupied by his widow, and his daughter Mariah lived there
until her death in 1888.

Placed on the National Register in 1972, the house became
a restaurant in 1980, named for Mariah Moore. The exterior
probably looks much as she knew it, and although the interior
has been changed greatly by the removal of walls both upstairs and down, it still has some original floors, mantels,
and woodwork. The collection of antiques and curiosities
added by owners Rick Kelley and David Sears contributes a
lighthearted touch downstairs, while the large combination
room upstairs, sporting a fireplace at each end and five big
windows across the front, is more formal.

The menu provides a wide selection, with vegetable, cheese,
meat and poultry appetizers, spectacular salads, hearty soups
and sandwiches. Entrées of steak, seafood, and pasta include
soup and salad, and are accompanied by a daily special, a
special soup of the day, and an unusual choice of egg dishes.
Gooey desserts like Mariah's Delight (hot fudge, nut brownie,
ice cream and whipped cream) should satisfy the sweetest
tooth.

Mariah's 1818 Restaurant, 801 State Street, Bowling Green, Kentucky
42101, is open from 11 a.m. to 10 p.m. Monday through Thursday, to 11

p.m. Friday and Saturday, with continuous service. (502)842-6878. Dress is casual, and reservations are requested for a party of six or more; all beverages are served. AE, MC, V. ($$)

MARIAH'S BROCCOLI AND CHEESE SOUP

1 bunch fresh broccoli
1 quart milk
½ pound Velveeta Cheese
½ teaspoon salt

½ teaspoon pepper
1 cup flour
1 cup butter
Salt and pepper

Cut florets from broccoli; place in saucepan and cover with water. Boil until just tender, drain, and chill.

In saucepan, place sliced broccoli stalks, covered with water, and boil until done. Purée stalks and remaining water in blender.

In saucepan, heat milk over low heat; cut cheese into small pieces and add to hot milk, stirring until cheese is melted. Add purée and florets.

Mix flour with butter until blended; drop by bits into broccoli mixture, and cook over medium heat until thickened, being careful not to boil. Season to taste. Serves six.

MARIAH'S CHICKEN AND FRUITS FIESTA

2 ounces melted butter
2 ounces Sauternes
2 Tablespoons brown
  sugar
One 8-ounce chicken
  breast, boned and
  skinned
4 strawberries, halved

½ banana, sliced ¼-inch
  thick
¼ fresh peach, sliced
  ¼-inch thick
1 ounce Grand Marnier
Grated orange rind for
  garnish

Heat butter, Sauternes, and sugar in skillet. Add chicken and sauté over medium heat about 4 minutes each side. Add fresh fruits and Grand Marnier and heat fruits through.

Place chicken breast on heated service plate and top with sauce. Garnish with grated orange rind. Serves one.

MARIAH'S CALIFORNIA CHICKEN SALAD

2 pounds boneless chicken
  breasts
¼ cup seedless white
  grapes, sliced
⅓ cup celery, chopped
Pinch salt
White pepper

4 Tablespoons sugar
½ cup mayonnaise
3 Tablespoons chopped
  parsley
Kentucky Bibb lettuce
Toasted almonds

Poach chicken breasts in water to cover until just done. Remove from liquid, cool, and dice small. Add remaining ingredients, except almonds and lettuce, and mix gently.

Line chilled plates with Kentucky Bibb lettuce; place two 3-ounce mounds of salad on lettuce. Top with 8 to 10 almonds and serve with a small fruit salad. Serves five.

MARIAH'S SHRIMP AND SCALLOPS ALFREDO

2 ounces butter, melted
3 ounces semi-dry Chablis
1 teaspoon minced garlic
3 Jumbo shrimp, peeled
  and deveined
3 ounces fresh bay scallops
¾ cup heavy cream

7 ounces fettucini, cooked
3 ounces Parmesan cheese
  freshly grated
2 Tablespoons chopped
  fresh chives
½ lemon, decoratively cut

Heat butter and Chablis in saucepan; add garlic, shrimp, and scallops. Sauté over medium heat 3 to 5 minutes, stirring occasionally.

Add cream and pasta, bring to a gentle boil, and stir until thickened. Pour onto heated plate and garnish with chives and lemon. Serve with shaker of grated Parmesan. Serves one.

THE PARAKEET CAFÉ
Bowling Green

IN THE MID-19TH CEN-
tury, as the importance of railroads became evident, there
was much competition among cities in south-central Kentucky to be on the route of the Louisville and Nashville Railroad. Bowling Green was successful, and the line to Nashville
opened in 1859. Trade was brisk between the two cities until
the beginning of the War Between the States closed the railroad in Tennessee, cutting off Bowling Green from the South.

On September 18, 1861, the Commonwealth of Kentucky,
previously holding to a position of neutrality, declared itself
for the Union; on that same day, Confederate forces invaded
Bowling Green. For five months, the city was occupied by
25,000 Confederate troops, and served as headquarters of the
Confederate Army of the West, under the command of General Albert Sidney Johnston, a Kentuckian.

Several fortifications built by the Confederates on hills surrounding Bowling Green were later captured and improved
by Union forces; portions of three still exist, and have been
placed on the National Register of Historic Places.

Just a block from Fountain Square, a little building of obscure origins has existed quietly for generations, serving as
livery stable, blacksmith shop, laundry, and delicatessen, and
used at one time for storage of caskets for a funeral home.

Since October of 1983, it has been Lon Durbin and Phil
Wilson's Parakeet Café, with food as clever and bright as
its decor. Who would believe this unprepossessing structure
could be so open and airy? Ceiling joists have been removed,
leaving stout chains to hold exposed-brick walls together; a
mezzanine and a side addition are used for seating, and the
effect is that of a European café.

Lon and Phil, who bring experience in several other fine
restaurants to The Parakeet, describe it as "a place where
you can be comfortable and have fun," offering "bistro-style
food," with predominantly grilled, baked, and light sautéed
items, and an emphasis on imagination and quality.

The lunch menu includes such classics as the hot Muffuletta
(ham, salami, Swiss and Mozzarella cheeses, spicy olive dressing), the Philly Cheesesteak Sandwich, and the Mushroom
and Artichoke Omelet, with fresh-cut fries. For dinner you

might try one of seven pastas, grilled Lemon-Ginger Chicken Breast, or New Orleans Barbecued Shrimp. There are nightly specials, chosen from "whatever's fresh," and such desserts as Mokoko Cheesecake and Crème Caramel, as well as a selection of homemade ice creams.

The Parakeet Café, 951 Chestnut Street, Bowling Green, Kentucky 42101, is open for lunch from 11 a.m. to 2 p.m., Monday through Saturday, and for dinner from 5 to 9:30 p.m. Monday through Thursday; and 5:30 to 10 p.m. Friday and Saturday. Light fare is served mid-afternoon and after dinner. (502)781-1538. The Parakeet is actually "in the middle of Chestnut Street, between Main and 10th." Dress is casual, all beverages are served, and reservations are accepted. AE, MC, V. ($$)

PARAKEET CAFÉ COUNTRY HAM PÂTÉ

1 Tablespoon Dijon mustard
4 dill pickle spears, chopped
4 green onions, chopped
¼ cup chopped fresh parsley
1 ½ teaspoons tarragon leaves
1 pound cooked country ham, coarsely chopped
Tabasco sauce

In a food processor fitted with the steel blade, process mustard, pickles, onions, parsley, and tarragon until finely chopped.

Add ham and Tabasco and process until very finely chopped—not totally ground.

Serve as spread with rye bread and pickles.

PARAKEET CAFÉ FETTUCINE CALIFORNIA

1 cup broccoli, lightly steamed
½ cup carrots, lightly steamed
1 small zucchini, sliced
½ cup sliced mushrooms
3 green onions, chopped
1 ½ cups heavy cream
⅓ pound fettucine, cooked al dente
Salt and pepper
½ to 1 teaspoon basil leaves
2 Tablespoons grated Parmesan cheese

In a non-stick skillet, bring vegetables and cream to boil. Add noodles and season with salt, pepper, and basil.

When noodles are heated, stir in Parmesan. More cream or more Parmesan may be added to correct consistency. Serves two.

PARAKEET CAFÉ CRÈME CARAMEL

2 ½ cups milk, scalded
¾ cup sugar
4 eggs
2 egg yolks
Dash of salt
½ teaspoon vanilla

Dash of nutmeg
Dash of cinnamon
Melted butter
6 Tablespoons brown sugar

In a bowl, mix sugar, eggs, yolks, salt, vanilla, nutmeg, and cinnamon. Add warm milk to egg mixture, and set aside.

Coat 6 ovenproof custard cups with melted butter. Press one tablespoon brown sugar into the bottom of each cup.

Divide milk/egg mixture among cups. Place cups in baking pan and add hot water to depth of 1 ½ inches. Bake at 350 degrees for one hour and 15 minutes.

Turn out warm custard on plate; it will make its own caramel sauce. Serves six.

BARNEY'S CALLAS GRILL
Owensboro

BOATMEN ON THE OHIO

river little thought that the landing they knew as "Yellow Banks" would someday be the largest town in Western Kentucky. Called "Rossborough" when it was laid out for the seat of Daviess County in 1815, it was renamed in 1817 for Colonel Abraham Owen, a hero of the War of 1812, who died at the battle of Tippecanoe.

Rapid industrial and mercantile growth of Owensboro during the late 19th and early 20th centuries can be attributed to railroad and river traffic, which brought in newcomers from many parts of the world.

One of these was Mike Callas, who alienated his family in Greece by coming to America in 1908 as a penniless 15-year-old. His adventures are almost a Horatio Alger success story: beginning by shining shoes, he rapidly earned the means to open an elegant confectionery. At the Progress Candy Store, he sold homemade candies and ice creams across a marble counter, and became one of Owensboro's best liked and most respected citizens.

After service during World War I, Callas returned to Owensboro and built a handsome new building next to the theatre on Frederica (locally pronounced FRED-ra-ka) Street to house his business. In 1921, the Callas Sweet Shop opened in the building, now a Kentucky Landmark, that still reflects the decor of those frivolous times.

Over the years, Mike Callas served as an officer or board member of nearly every charitable or service organization in the city, and when he visited his home in Greece in 1937, he was received as an honored guest. In 1960, he turned his business over to longtime friends Barney and Wilma Elliott.

Barney had started behind a drugstore counter at the age of 16, and Wilma had worked at the Callas Sweet shop from 1929 to 1934. While Wilma raised their family, Barney had a series of restaurants in Owensboro and nearby Morganfield.

They determined from the beginning to leave the Art Deco interior and the 1940's porcelain front of the Callas Building intact, and to serve "old-time foods like Mother taught me," Wilma said. The expanded menu was an immediate success.

Barney's Callas Grill is now run by their youngest son,

Jerry, who uses many of the same recipes. Lunchtime crowds swarm to Barney's for chicken pot pie, fried chicken (Wednesdays), REAL mashed potatoes, and fresh vegetables in season. Barney's Special (a hamburger through the garden with homemade french fries and cole slaw) isn't even on the menu, but remains popular. Homemade raisin, chocolate, and coconut pies are available every day, with butterscotch and chess as "surprises."

Barney's Callas Grill, 420 Frederica Street, Owensboro, Kentucky 43201, is open from 6 a.m. to 3 p.m. Monday through Friday. (502)683-2363. Dress is casual, and credit cards and reservations are not accepted. ($)

BARNEY'S FRUIT SALAD

2 eggs
¾ cup sugar
Juice of 2 lemons
3 bananas, sliced

1 cup crushed pineapple, drained
1 cup shredded coconut

In saucepan, beat eggs and sugar together, slowly add lemon juice, and beat well. Cook until thick; cool. Add fruit and refrigerate until served.

BARNEY'S CHICKEN POT PIE

Pie crust dough
1 large fryer chicken
1 stick butter or margarine
3 Tablespoons flour
4 cups chicken broth
1 cup milk
4 ribs celery, diced
One 10-ounce package
   frozen peas, cooked by
   package directions

One 10-ounce package
   frozen carrots
¼ teaspoon pepper
Salt to taste
Melted butter

In large pot, stew chicken in water to cover until tender. Remove chicken from broth, reserving broth, and pull meat from bones, discarding skin and bones. Dice meat and set aside.

In large pan, melt butter, stir in flour, then add broth from chicken with milk. Cook over medium heat, stirring constantly, until a moderately thick sauce is made.

Place chicken in large, deep casserole dish, with drained peas, carrots, and celery. Add sauce, pepper, and salt, and mix well. Cover with uncooked pie crust and brush with butter.

Bake at 350 degrees until crust is golden brown and mixture is bubbly.

BARNEY'S SCALLOPED EGGPLANT

1 large eggplant
1 cup half and half cream
1 cup milk

2 cups cracker crumbs
1 stick butter, melted
Salt and pepper

Peel eggplant and dice in 1-inch cubes. Boil in small amount salted water until tender, and drain well. Add cream and milk to eggplant; stir in cracker crumbs, butter, and salt and pepper to taste.

Place in casserole dish and sprinkle small amount of butter on top. Bake at 375 degrees until brown.

BARNEY'S RAISIN PIE

One 9-inch baked pie shell
1 ½ cups brown sugar
3 Tablespoons flour
3 eggs, divided

1 ½ cups raisins
½ stick butter
4 Tablespoons sugar

In saucepan, cook sugar, flour, egg yolks, raisins and 1½ cups water over medium heat until mixture is thick. Stir in butter and pour into baked pie shell.

Make meringue of egg whites and sugar (beat egg whites until dry, gradually add sugar and continue beating until sugar is dissolved.) Spread meringue over pie, being careful to seal edges, and bake until meringue is slightly brown. Serves eight.

BARTHOLOMEW'S
Hopkinsville

$\mathbf{I}$N 1796, A NORTH CARO-
linian named Bartholomew Wood ended his search for land
in the western part of Kentucky, and erected a log cabin
near The Rock Spring, a landmark not far from the crossing
of the Russellville trail and the Little River.

In this fertile Pennyroyal (pronounced, and often spelled,
"Pennyrile') region of Kentucky, things were happening fast.
Within the next year, a new county was established, named
for Patrick Henry's brother-in-law, Colonel William Christian, a Revolutionary War hero killed by Indians while at-
tempting to settle the area that is now Louisville.

The Christian County seat was to be between the forks of
Little River at The Rock Spring, and Bartholomew Wood donated five acres of land for the public buildings. The town
that grew up around this center, originally named Elizabeth,
was renamed for General Samuel Hopkins in 1804, and is
familiarly known as "Hoptown."

Bartholomew Wood is commemorated by two monuments:
one a statue in Hopkinsville's pioneer cemetary, the other
a handsome new restaurant on the site of his original cabin.

There is little of the pioneer spirit in Bartholomew's, however; the building it occupies, a brick, terra cotta and stone
structure of Romanesque architecture, was built in 1894 as
The Racket Store, which sold buggies and general merchan-
dise. The site was later used by hardware stores and an auto
parts store.

In 1982, a sensitive restoration adapted the lower portion
as the dining room, and the mezzanine, left from a 1920's
remodeling, as the bar; upper floors are still used for office
space. The open, airy restaurant that resulted is filled with
plants, light, and interesting photographs of Hopkinsville's
past. There's even a picture of Bartholomew T. Wood, son
of the founder, and a copy of the original deed to the property.

Bartholomew's approach to food is innovative and caring.
"We try to start with the best ingredients," said part owner
and General Manager Colby MacQuarrie. "In Hopkinsville,
you're dealing with a lot of good home cooks and competing
with that."

Soups, quiches and omelets reflect available fresh ingredients, and salads, served with hot croissants, are unusual combinations. Ground chuck burgers with various toppings are on egg batter buns with sharp Cheddar cheese and french fries cut from fresh potatoes, and entrées are interestingly prepared and generously served. Daily specials are usually seafood, and homemade desserts and dessert drinks are rich and innovative. Don't miss the Strawberry Shortcake drink and the Black Bottom Cheesecake!

Bartholomew's, 914 S. Main Street (corner of 10th), Hopkinsville, Kentucky 42240, is open for lunch Monday through Saturday from 11 a.m. to 2:30 p.m. and for dinner Monday through Thursday from 5 to 9:30 p.m., until 11 p.m. on Friday and Saturday. (502)886-5768. Dress is informal, all beverages are served, and reservations are accepted. There is a special menu for children. AE, MC, V. ($$)

BARTHOLOMEW'S LOADED POTATO SOUP

2 cups coarsely chopped celery
2 cups coarsely chopped white onion
2 cups 1-inch sliced carrots
¾ teaspoon white pepper
2 quarts chicken stock
2 cups 1 ½" cubed potato
1 cup whipping cream
½ cup flour, blended with
2 Tablespoons butter

In large pan combine vegetables, pepper, and chicken stock. Boil until vegetables are tender; add potato and cream and simmer 15 or 20 minutes. Add some of flour/butter mixture to thicken; all may not be needed. Simmer to cook flour. Correct seasonings and add salt if necessary. Serves 10 to 12.

BARTHOLOMEW'S CHICKEN VELVET SOUP

6 ounces (1 ½ sticks) butter
¾ cup flour
1 cup milk
1 cup heavy cream
6 cups chicken stock
2 cups chopped cooked chicken
1 teaspoon salt
1 teaspoon white pepper
1 teaspoon Dijon mustard
Fresh parsley, chopped, for garnish

172

In a saucepan, blend butter and flour and cook over medium heat for 2 minutes. Heat milk, cream, and stock, and add a little at a time to butter/flour mixture, stirring, until mixture is smooth and thickened. When it begins to boil, add chicken and seasonings. Sprinkle bowls of soup with chopped parsley. Serves eight.

BARTHOLOMEW'S BLACK BOTTOM CHEESECAKE

2 cups chocolate wafer crumbs
4 ounces (½ stick) butter, melted
¾ teaspoon cinnamon
2 ¼ pounds cream cheese, at room temperature
1 ½ cups sugar
4 eggs
¼ cup green crème de menthe
¼ teaspoon peppermint extract
¼ teaspoon salt
½ cup semi-sweet chocolate chips
¼ cup sour cream

Preheat oven to 250 degrees. Grease and flour 9" springform pan. Combine chocolate crumbs, melted butter and cinnamon in large bowl and blend until mixture can be packed easily. Press into pan, covering bottom only, and set aside. In large bowl, combine cream cheese, sugar, and eggs and mix well. Stir in crème de menthe, peppermint extract and salt, and blend smooth. Pour into prepared pan, add chocolate chips and sour cream, and stir just to mix. Bake 45 minutes, turn off heat and leave in oven for 60 minutes with door closed. Refrigerate cheesecake in pan for at least 4 hours. To serve, run knife around side of pan and remove springform rim. Serves eight.

SKYLINE SUPPER CLUB
Hopkinsville

THE RAPID 19TH-CENtury development of Christian County, based on agriculture, caused the population to double; Hopkinsville became one of the major cities of the Pennyroyal. The county is known for dark air-cured tobacco, a heavy type used for chewing tobacco and cigar filler, and marketing of this and other agricultural products was facilitated by nearby steamboat traffic. This, with a ready supply of labor, aided in economic recovery after the War Between the States.

Later, when the Louisville and Nashville Railroad connected Hopkinsville with important markets in Tennessee and along the Ohio River, Hopkinsville continued to grow.

Many businesses and houses were built during this period of expansion and although the Greek Revival style remained popular in the county until the turn of the century, elements of Gothic Revival and Italianate design are to be seen in many buildings in Hopkinsville. They frequently exhibit interesting external decoration rather than slavish devotion to a stylistic form, giving Hopkinsville houses of this period an unusual charm.

The large, L-shaped brick structure that houses the Skyline Supper Club has Gothic gables and a sweeping moorish gingerbread-trimmed porch, and was probably built in the 1880's on the site of an earlier building. It may, however, be a large addition to the house shown on the deed before 1865. Whatever its age, it is gracious and comfortable, well adapted for its use as a public building.

In 1958 it became the clubhouse for a country club, but stood empty for seven years after the club closed in 1970. Rescued by Frank and Peggy Walls in 1977, it again serves golfers— now on the municipal course—and others in search of a romantic dinner.

Entering the 8-foot high, white poplar front door, the visitor is confronted with a curving staircase; a small dining room on the right and the lounge on the left are original rooms, but the main dining room toward the rear is part of the 1958 renovation, which expanded the former back porch into a spacious room with multiple floor levels. Here, gas logs flicker on wintery nights, and a new glass atrium overlooks the swimming pool.

Prime Rib is a specialty at the Skyline Supper Club; there are also steaks, a dozen seafood entrées (including lobster), chicken, and country ham, all accompanied by salad (try the spinach with bacon, tomato, and hot vinaigrette), a choice of five potatoes (the German fries with green peppers and onions are delicious) and hot bread. Plenty of appetizers and desserts are available to lenghten a leisurely meal as you watch the sun set across the golf course.

The Skyline Supper Club, 1724 Marie Drive, Hopkinsville, Kentucky 42240, is just off Skyline Drive, and is open for dinner only, from 5 to 10 p.m. Tuesday through Thursday, and until 10:30 Friday and Saturday. (502)886-9203. Dress is informal and all beverages are available; reservations are accepted and are preferred for groups of six or more. AE, MC, V. ($$)

SKYLINE SUPPER CLUB FRENCH FRIED EGGPLANT

1 large eggplant	1 cup cracker meal
1 cup flour	Cooking oil
1 cup milk	Seasoned salt

Peel eggplant and cut lengthwise into thin strips, about ½" to ¾" wide. Dip eggplant strips first in flour, then milk, then roll in cracker meal.

Drop strips into oil heated to 350 degrees, and cook for ten to 12 minutes, or until golden brown. Remove strips from oil, drain on paper towels, and sprinkle with seasoned salt. Serve with following Sweet and Sour Appetizer Sauce.
Note: oil that has been used several times will ensure golden brown color; fresh oil will produce a pale color.

SKYLINE SUPPER CLUB SWEET AND SOUR APPETIZER SAUCE

2 Tablespoons cornstarch	¼ cup sugar
2 Tablespoons soy sauce	1 ½ teaspoons salt
1 ½ cups chicken stock, divided	¾ teaspoon powdered ginger
½ cup vinegar	
½ cup Meier's Blackberry Wine	

In a saucepan, combine cornstarch, soy sauce, and ½ cup chicken broth to make a paste; add other ingredients and mix thoroughly. Simmer, stirring constantly, until mixture thickens.

Serve with bite-size appetizers, breaded shrimp, egg rolls or cocktail franks. Yields about 2 ½ cups.

SKYLINE SUPPER CLUB BRISKET OF BEEF WITH HOT SAUCE

1 large beef brisket

In large pot over low heat, cook brisket in water to cover for three to four hours. Cool brisket in broth, remove, and refrigerate overnight. Slice thinly while cold, and serve with the following hot sauce.

Sauce:

Sugar	**Onion flakes**
Vinegar	**Horseradish (optional)**
1 egg, lightly beaten	

In small bowl, combine equal parts of sugar and vinegar. Add egg, onion flakes, and horseradish, if used, and blend thoroughly. Store in refrigerator, covered.

SKYLINE SUPPER CLUB PLUM SUNDAE DESSERT

Plums, Santa Rosa variety preferred	**Sugar to taste**
	Vanilla ice cream

Remove seeds from plums. In a saucepan, cook plums in a small amount of water three to five minutes, or until tender. Slip skins from plums, and purée plum pulp in a food processor. Add sugar to taste, and serve over vanilla ice cream.

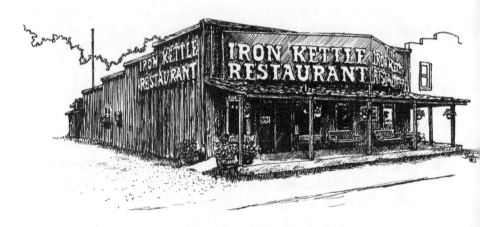

THE IRON KETTLE
Grand Rivers

WHEN THOMAS LAWSON,
a Boston businessman and promoter, came to the land between the Tennessee and Cumberland rivers in the mid
1870's, it was an area of ironworks. Oxen hauled wood to
be burned for charcoal needed by the furnaces; ore was trans-
ported by wagonloads and pig iron was shipped on the rivers.

Excited by the thriving industry and a new railroad, Lawson and his backers founded the new town of Grand Rivers,
and built another furnace, handsome houses, and a business
section called "The Boston Block." Incorporating an entire
city block of stores and offices and a hotel, it was an important
part of the town that was intended to rival Pittsburgh.

Local ore was inferior, however, and more easily mined
ore discovered in northern Alabama doomed the local industry. Lawson left quietly one night in 1918, abandoning his
project, and unemployed ironworkers found work in the bur-
geoning gravel business.

Each time that misfortune came to Grand Rivers, better
times followed; even the disastrous 1937 flood ultimately resulted in the two lakes that now provide tourism for the entire
area. Kentucky Lake, Lake Barkley and The Land Between
the Lakes attract thousands of people each year for fishing
and recreation in scenic waters and unspoiled woodland.

Although much of The Boston Block was burned in 1940,
the City Hall, at one end, and The Iron Kettle restaurant,
at the other, have rebuilt. Hungry fisherfolk know The Iron
Kettle as the home of "real country cooking," provided for
16 years by Mabel Nash and a hardworking crew.

People from every country in the world, as many as a thousand a day on summer weekends, have served themselves
repeatedly with The Iron Kettle's bounty. Those unfamiliar
with such regional foods as hominy, pea salad, and chicken
gizzard stew have been surprised and pleased, have taken
"just a little more," then have brought their friends.

Two old-fashioned wood stoves, now heated by gas, serve
as buffets, with homemade yeast and corn breads in the ovens
and choices of meats and vegetables on top. On a typical day,
chicken and dumplings, ham and beans, and fried chicken
are accompanied by broccoli casserole, baked beans, baked

apples, turnip greens, butterbeans, and stewed tomatoes, with a 50-item salad bar and peach and apple cobbler for dessert. Homemade bread is available to take out, if you're still hungry.

There is fried fish evenings and weekends, seafood on Friday nights, and hearty breakfasts to order in the mornings. This is the place to bring a real outdoors appetite!

The Iron Kettle, Grand Rivers, Kentucky 42045, is open from the first of March until late fall (depending upon weather) from 6 a.m. to 8:30 p.m., seven days a week. (502)362-8396. Grand Rivers is between Lakes Barkley and Kentucky, just off I-24. Reservations are necessary only for parties; personal checks are accepted; no credit cards. ($)

IRON KETTLE COLE SLAW

1 cup white vinegar
½ cup sugar
½ teaspoon garlic salt
Average head of cabbage,
    shredded

½ carrot, chopped
½ green pepper, chopped
½ small onion, chopped

Measure vinegar, add sugar and salt, and stir into vegetables. Chill thoroughly before serving. Keeps in refrigerator up to two weeks. Serves eight to ten.

IRON KETTLE HOT PEPPER CORNBREAD

2 cups milk
2 eggs
½ cup sugar
2 cups self-rising white
    cornmeal

½ cup hot jalapeno
    peppers, chopped while
    wearing gloves
1 cup grated Cheddar
    cheese

Grease and heat 9-inch black iron skillet until very hot.
In large bowl, mix milk, eggs, sugar, and cornmeal. Stir in peppers and cheese. Pour into hot skillet and bake at 400 degrees until firm and crusty around edges. Serves eight. Note: use extreme caution when handling peppers.

IRON KETTLE CHICKEN AND DUMPLINGS

1 large chicken, cut up
Salt
4 cups flour
1 teaspoon salt

3 eggs, beaten
2 chicken bouillon cubes
Yellow food coloring,
    optional

In large pot, place chicken with salted water to cover; cook over medium heat until chicken is tender. Remove chicken from broth and set aside to cool. Reserve broth.

In bowl, mix flour with 1 teaspoon salt, eggs, and 1 cup broth from chicken. Stir until stiff; knead as if it were bread dough, then roll paper thin. Cut into 1" x 4" strips.

Return pot of broth to heat; add water to make one gallon, bouillon, and coloring, if used. Bring to boil.

Remove chicken from bones and cut into bite-sized pieces.

Drop dumpling strips into boiling broth a few at a time while stirring. "Boil until you know they're done," said Mrs. Nash. Taste to be sure. Remove dumplings with slotted spoon, combine with chicken, and serve.

THE NINTH STREET HOUSE
Paducah

IN 1795, GENERAL GEORGE Rogers Clark was awarded substantial acreage in what is now southwestern Kentucky for his service during the Revolutionary War. After his death, his brother, General William Clark, inherited a tract at the confluence of the Ohio and Tennessee rivers, containing a village named Pekin.

William Clark, noted for his exploration of the Far West with Meriwether Lewis, renamed the settlement in memory of friendly Indian Chief Paduke, and laid out the streets of a larger town on the site. Only 50 miles from the Mississippi, Paducah's early success was tied to river traffic, and the town grew as an industrial and commercial center.

A great-nephew of the Clarks, George Wallace, commissioned famed Kentucky architect Brinton B. Davis to design his winter home in Paducah's "Lower Town" in 1886. The resulting large Queen Anne-style house survived threatened demolition in the early 1970's, and became a restaurant in 1974. Rescue of this important landmark by present owners Curtis and Norma Grace spearheaded restoration in a 30-block area; the historic district of Lower Town was placed on The National Register in 1982.

At The Ninth Street House, a piazza curves around the octagonal corner tower, and is used for guest seating in pleasant weather, extending the welcome of the handsome hall. Interiors, restored to original glory, have the dark woodwork, stained and beveled glass, and elegance of the Victorian era, enhanced by antiques of the period, including an 1865 Steinway played on weekend nights. Beneath the decorative mantels in each dining room fires are lighted on cool evenings, adding to the feeling of candlelit intimacy.

The "Classic Southern Cooking" at The Ninth Street House showcases the creative genius of owner/chef Curtis Grace in menus that change weekly, of 5 or 6 entrées, mostly original. Trout, prime rib, and lamb are constants, but other entrées vary daily.

"I like to come up with new ideas," Grace said, "and you have to start with good ingredients." He shops daily for fresh foods, "But I do overcook string beans—I like to cook them until they turn purple." Other vegetables are crisp and cooked to order, seafoods are fresh daily, and breads, dressings, and ice creams are homemade, as are marvelous desserts that feature crisp pastry, fresh fruit, and gobs of whipped cream.

Luncheon fare includes the soup of the day, unusual sandwiches, California Chicken Salad, an enormous Chef's Salad, and a Daily Special. The iced tea, a house secret, has been called "the best in the world!"

The Ninth Street House, 323 Ninth Street, Paducah 42001, is open from 11 a.m. to 2 p.m. for lunch, Tuesday through Saturday, and for dinner from 6 to 8:30 p.m., Tuesday through Thursday. Friday and Saturday dinner is served in two seatings, with the last reservation taken at 9 p.m. (502)442-9019. Dress is informal, and reservations are suggested; all beverages are served. DC, MC, V. ($$)

NINTH STREET HOUSE CONGEALED SPINACH SALAD WITH CRABMEAT DRESSING

9 ounces lime gelatin
6 Tablespoons vinegar
1 ½ cups mayonnaise
3 cups cottage cheese
4 Tablespoons minced
onion

1 cup diced celery
Three 10-ounce packages
frozen chopped spinach,
thawed, drained, and
squeezed dry
Tomato wedges for garnish

Dissolve gelatin in 3 cups boiling water; add ½ cup cold water and vinegar, then all other ingredients, and pour into 9″ x 13″ pan that has been coated with mayonnaise. Refrigerate until congealed. Cut into squares, garnish with tomato wedges, and serve with crabmeat dressing. Serves 12 to 15.

Crabmeat dressing:
3 cups mayonnaise
¾ cup chili sauce
6 Tablespoons horseradish

½ large onion, chopped
Tabasco (optional)
2 cups flaked crabmeat

Mix all ingredients except crabmeat. Fold in crabmeat, and spoon over squares of Congealed Spinach Salad.

184

NINTH STREET HOUSE DUSTY'S RED MUSHROOM SOUP

1 pound fresh mushrooms, sliced
1 onion, chopped
2 cloves garlic, minced
Olive oil
1 Tablespoon butter

3 Tablespoons tomato paste
3 cups chicken broth
Sweet vermouth to taste
Parmesan cheese, grated

Sauté mushrooms, onion, and garlic in olive oil and butter. Add remaining ingredients and simmer about 10 minutes. Pour into bowls and dust with cheese. Yields about a quart.

NINTH STREET HOUSE SAUTEED SAUSAGE AND GRITS

4 cups chicken stock
1 cup quick grits
½ cup cornmeal
1 pound bulk sausage, sautéed and drained

3 eggs, beaten
Salt, pepper, and cayenne
CLARIFIED butter or oil
Maple syrup

Cook grits in rapidly boiling chicken stock until thick; add cornmeal, sausage, eggs and seasonings to taste. Place in loaf pan and refrigerate overnight. Slice and sauté in CLARIFIED butter or oil; serve with maple syrup. Serves four.

NINTH STREET HOUSE BUTTERMILK CHESS PIE

One 9-inch unbaked pie shell
2 Tablespoons flour
1 cup sugar
⅔ cup buttermilk

4 eggs, beaten
1 stick butter, melted
Pinch of salt
1 teaspoon vanilla

In large bowl, mix flour and sugar together, combine with buttermilk, eggs, butter, salt and vanilla. Mix by hand; mixer will give a different texture.

Pour into pie shell and bake at 325 degrees until golden brown and firm, about 45 minutes to one hour. Serves six to eight.

YESTERDAY'S
Paducah

PADUCAH'S LOWER

town, annexed to the city in 1836, was so called because it was downstream from "Old Town," originally laid out by General William Clark. It was the first residential section of Paducah, and handsome homes—some meant only for summer use—were constructed there for prominent citizens.

During the War between the States, the sympathy of most Paducah residents was with the South, and with many men away in the war, Federal forces invaded the area without a shot. In 1861, General U.S. Grant, with 5,000 men, built a pontoon bridge across the Ohio River from Illinois. The Union held the city unchallenged for nearly three years, occupying the ruins of the burned Marine Hospital, fortifying it and naming it "Fort Anderson."

On Good Friday in 1864, 1,800 Confederate cavalrymen, led by General Nathan Bedford Forrest, attacked the fort, under the command of Colonel Stephen B. Hicks. The fort's breastworks defied attack, so Confederate sharpshooters fired down into the fort from second-story windows of nearby houses.

Unsuccessful, the Confederates retreated, and all houses within firing range of the fort were burned. Few ante-bellum structures remain in Lower Town, for that reason, but construction after the war resulted in a neighborhood of unusual interest. It was placed on The National Register in 1982.

The building that now houses Yesterday's restaurant, believed to be the oldest saloon in Western Kentucky, was built on the site of an even earlier tavern and stagecoach stop. The tavern had a seamy reputation around the turn of the century, when legend says a brothel operated upstairs. That part of the building was used for the manufacture of illegal beverages during Prohibition; the tavern downstairs was a popular speakeasy.

By contrast, Yesterday's is tame, indeed, and although today's clientele is quite respectable, some of the old flavor remains in the friendly, relaxed atmosphere. Old local tile floors and wainscot in the front room are colorful and novel, and the cozy inner rooms with exposed brick and rough-sawn wood serve as a gallery for local artist Steven Estes. An enclosed tropical garden is used for warm-weather cookouts.

Under the direction of Jerry Sanders, part owner and manager, Yesterday's serves what he terms "fun food, with a variety of everything—pasta, crepes, omelets, quiches—whatever your appetite is, there's something for it on the menu."

Chicken and fish dishes are popular, as are special salads and burgers, with oversized portions the norm, and desserts—like Mud Sundae (fudge brownie, vanilla ice cream, Bailey's Irish Cream Liqueur)—are clever and rich.

Yesterday's, 701 Park Avenue, Paducah, Kentucky 42011, is open from 11 a.m. to 10 p.m. Monday through Thursday, to 11 p.m. on Friday and Saturday, with continuous service. (502)443-6216. Dress is casual, all beverages are served, and reservations are not necessary except for parties of ten or more. A special menu is available for children. MC, V. ($)

YESTERDAY'S CHICKEN TETRAZZINI

Cooked rice or noodles
1 whole cooked chicken,
about 4 to 5 pounds
Butter for sautéeing
½ cup chopped green
onions

¾ cup mushrooms, sliced
¼ cup white wine
2 teaspoons garlic salt

Pull chicken apart, removing skin and bones. Cut into strips and set aside. In medium skillet, sauté vegetables, add wine and garlic salt, and simmer.

Divide rice or noodles onto four serving plates, distribute chicken on top, and pour sauce over all. Serves four.

YESTERDAY'S HOUSE DRESSING

½ cup sugar
1 ⅔ cup vegetable oil
3 ½ ounces red wine
vinegar

½ cup + 2 Tablespoons
catsup
2 Tablespoons bacon
crumbles

Blend together all ingredients; shake or stir before using each time—it will keep indefinitely in refrigerator. Yields about 3 cups.

YESTERDAY'S CHICKEN SICILIAN

Cooked rice or noodles
1 whole cooked chicken
Butter for sautéeing
1 cup chopped cooked
  potato

½ cup grated Parmesan
  cheese
¼ cup wine
2 teaspoons garlic salt

Pull chicken apart, removing skin and bones. Cut into strips and set aside. In medium skillet, sauté potato in butter, add cheese, wine, and garlic, and simmer.

Divide rice or noodles onto four serving plates, distribute chicken on top, and pour sauce over all. Serves four.

YESTERDAY'S SEAFOOD GUMBO

¾ cup flour
¾ cup shortening or oil
2 ¼ teaspoons garlic
  powder
½ cup diced onion
½ cup chopped bell pepper
½ cup chopped celery
1 ¼ pounds crabmeat,
  shredded
1 ½ pounds raw shrimp,
  peeled

½ cup chopped fresh
  parsley
1 ½ teaspoons thyme
2 to 3 bay leaves
9 ounces tomato sauce
⅜ pound cut okra
½ pint raw oysters
  (optional)
Salt and pepper
Tabasco sauce

In large pot, blend flour with shortening or oil over medium heat until brown, at least 15 or 20 minutes. Stir in garlic powder, onion, pepper and celery, and cook until tender. Add seafood, except oysters, spices, tomato sauce, and 3 quarts water, and cook about an hour. Add okra and cook an additional 30 to 45 minutes. The last 15 minutes of cooking, add oysters, if used. Season with salt, pepper, and Tabasco to taste. Serve in soup bowls with French bread. Serves about 16.

C.C. COHEN
Paducah

WHEN PADUCAH WAS IN-
corporated in 1830, there was already a site for a market
house, deeded to the city by William Clark in 1827. A succes-
sion of market buildings were built on the spot, the third
and final one a massive brick structure erected in 1905.

Over the years, this central location was where city people
and farmers met to trade fresh produce, meats, and eggs, to
discuss politics and daily happenings. A substantial business
district developed around the Market House, but as the city
grew, neighborhood markets replaced the central one, and
the Market House was closed in 1955.

When it was scheduled for demolition to make room for
a parking lot in the early 1960's, a group of women volunteers,
the Civic Beautification Board, stepped in to save the Market
House. Through their efforts, it was renovated in 1965 to
become an art gallery, a museum, and a theatre, and was
placed on the National Register of Historic Places in 1978.
These tireless ladies initiated an awareness of preservation
in Paducah that has resulted in recognition of four historic
areas and numerous individual historic sites.

Next door to the Market House, the Cohen building, built
about 1870, was used for hardware, clothing, and drygoods
stores before housing a liquor dealer and distillery in the
early 1900's.

In 1921, Ike Cohen bought the building for his pawnshop,
and his family lived on the upper floors. When the last member of the Cohen family died in 1980, the building was adapted
by present owner Charles Taylor for its present use as a restaurant, which took its name from the family that had occupied the building longest.

Few changes have been made to the exterior of the structure; metal window hoods and cornice dominate the upper
floors, and the lower floor is almost entirely glass.

The interior, flooded with light, has different floor levels
to establish seating areas, and the high ceiling has an opening
to the second-floor lounge.

A newspaper-style menu offers selections from the oyster
bar, omelets and potatoes with various fillings, soups and salads, sandwiches and burgers. Entrées emphasize beef, seafood,

and chicken, with "Dynamic Specials" through the week, seasonal menus for summer and winter, and an additional weekend specialty menu. Unusual drinks, "theatrical" coffees from around the world, and desserts such as deep-fried ice cream and Mama's American Apple Pie assure a meal that truly has "something for everyone."

C.C. Cohen, 101-105 South Second Street, Paducah, Kentucky 42001, is open 11 a.m. to 10 p.m. Monday through Thursday, to 11 p.m. on weekends, with continuous service; lounge (with an age limit of 21 or older) is open until 2:30 a.m. on weekends. (502)442-6391. Dress is casual, all beverages are served, and no reservations are taken. There is a special menu for children. AE, MC, V.($$)

C.C. COHEN'S BAKED GULF OYSTERS COHEN

3 dozen fresh shucked
  oysters on the half shell
3 cups chopped broccoli
1 cup chopped stuffed
  green olives

⅛ cup lemon juice
¼ cup dried parsley flakes
One ¾-inch cut of Cheddar
  cheese for each oyster

Place oysters on large baking sheet.

Combine broccoli, olives, lemon juice, and parsley flakes and spoon on each oyster, topping with cheese. Bake for 25 minutes at 400 degrees. Serve with lemons and cocktail sauce. Serves four to six.

C.C. COHEN SCALLOPS JAMBALAYA

10 cups cooked hot rice
8 to 10 slices bacon,
  chopped
1 large tomato, chopped
2 ½ pounds fresh scallops
½ cup chopped ham
¼ cup chopped celery
¼ cup chopped green
  onions
¼ cup chopped white
  onion

¼ cup chopped bell pepper
1 cup tomato sauce
¼ cup olive oil
¼ cup melted butter
2 teaspoons
  Worcestershire sauce
1 teaspoon Tabasco sauce
1 teaspoon sugar
Garlic salt
Oregano
Green onions for garnish

In large pan, simmer bacon on low heat for 15 minutes or until bacon fat is dissolved. Add chopped tomato and simmer an additional 6 to 7 minutes, stirring occasionally. Add remaining ingredients, garlic salt and oregano to taste, and bring to a boil.

Reduce heat and simmer 15 minutes. Serve over hot rice, garnished with green onions. Serves six.

C.C. COHEN'S HOUSE DRESSING

1 pound sugar
1 ¼ quarts vegetable oil
3 cups red wine vinegar
16 ounces catsup

½ teaspoon basil
6 strips bacon, cooked and crumbled

Combine all ingredients. Shake or stir well before serving.

C.C. COHEN'S IKE COHEN'S "VANISHING POINT"

Recipe and anecdote as given by General Manager Marty Keleman:

"Six ounces vodka or gin poured over ice in a heavy beer goblet, garnished with three jumbo olives. Just whisper the word 'vermouth' while stirring.

It is said by many that Mr. Cohen's spectre inhabits the upper floors of his old property. Vodka and gin bottles are repeatedly about 6 ounces short after being marked by myself and Charles Taylor, the present owner. Consequently, we invented a drink for Mr. Ike."

JEREMIAH'S
Paducah

IN THE MIDDLE OF THE 19th century, Paducah was already an important regional marketing center, with a substantial river port and prospering banks. Railroads began negotiations for Paducah's trade in the early 1850's, and in 1856, it was named a third-class city by the Kentucky Legislature. By 1860, it had grown into a thriving town of 4,590 citizens.

Growth came to a standstill during the War Between the States, but in the decade that followed, industrial development increased rapidly. In addition to the largest boat-building operation on the Ohio River, ease of river and rail distribution encouraged the establishment of foundries, lumberyards, distilleries, breweries, and manufactories of tobacco-related products.

The successful new industries created a need for financial institutions, and between 1870 and 1890, a number of banks were established. In the 1870's, the City National Bank constructed a building that they occupied until relocating to a 10-story "skyscraper" in 1910. Used by the Mechanics' Trust and Savings Bank until 1930, then by several stores, the building became a restaurant in 1979.

The word "Bank" on the pediment high above the street is the last vestige of the building's origin; the large, green frog beside the door is a key to Jeremiah's humorous, relaxed decor. Rustic, rough cut wood and exposed brick on the interior are lighted by Victorian reproduction lamps, and frogs are everywhere, from tiny ceramic figurines to enormous statues.

Owners Tom and Martha Sanders have worked hard to make Jeremiah's a friendly, unusual place in which to dine— or even to cook your own meal! There is no kitchen, and all hot food is prepared on a huge charcoal grill in the center of the restaurant. You can watch while meats and vegetables (and frog legs, of course) are grilled, or you can do your own and save a dollar.

"Consider us a people's restaurant," Martha Sanders said. "We're not fast food, and not gourmet, but everything's fresh and good, and we try to give the public good value and good quality."

Jeremiah's offers something different nearly every night. On Friday, there's Killarney mixture: shrimp and corn on the cob plunged into a boiling pot full of seasonings to order. Other specials are barbecued chicken (Thursday), and "Three Drink Marinade" (have three drinks, and your meat is marinated, grilled, and ready to eat). Kabobs, Orange Roughy, and steaks you select from a glass cooler are always available, with a choice of salads and desserts. Portions are generous, and you can take home the leftovers for a second good meal from Jeremiah's.

Jeremiah's, 225 Broadway, Paducah, Kentucky 42001, is open for dinner only, Monday through Saturday from 5 p.m. "Until the coals are gone." (502)443-3991. All beverages are available, dress is casual, and reservations are suggested for a party of eight or more. All items on the menu are the same price, and children under 5 years are served free. MC, V, ($$)

JEREMIAH'S FRENCH DRESSING

½ large onion, chopped fine
¼ cup + 2 Tablespoons vinegar
1 Tablespoon salt
¼ teaspoon red pepper
½ teaspoon dry mustard

Juice of ½ large lemon
2 cups oil
1 cup tomato catsup
¾ cup sugar

Blend all ingredients thoroughly; keeps indefinitely in sealed jar in refrigerator. Yields about a quart.

JEREMIAH'S FRUIT WITH HONEY SAUCE
Melon balls or fruit of any kind; serve with following Sauce:

⅓ cup honey
⅓ cup vinegar
⅓ cup sugar
1 teaspoon paprika

1 teaspoon dry mustard
1 teaspoon celery seed
1 teaspoon lemon juice (optional)
1 cup vegetable oil

In a blender, mix honey, vinegar, sugar, spices, and lemon juice, if used. Very, very slowly, drip oil into the mixture with blender at high speed. When well mixed, pour into a jar and seal tightly. Keeps indefinitely in refrigerator. Yields about a pint.

JEREMIAH'S CARAMEL PIE

One 9-inch baked pie shell
1 cup sugar, divided
¼ teaspoon butter
2 Tablespoons flour OR
  cornstarch

1 cup milk
3 egg yolks (reserve whites
  for meringue)
1 Tablespoon butter
1 teaspoon vanilla

In iron skillet, place ¼ cup sugar with ¼ teaspoon butter, and set aside.

In saucepan, combine ¾ cup sugar with flour. Add milk to moisten, beat in egg yolks one at a time, and stir in remaining milk. Over low heat, stirring constantly, cook until hot, but not boiling. Remove from heat and set aside.

Stir sugar and butter over medium heat until melted and brown. Drip into milk mixture, stirring constantly over low heat until thickened. Remove from heat, add butter and vanilla, and cool before pouring into crust. Cover pie with meringue (see below), and bake at 375 degrees about 15 minutes.

Meringue:
3 egg whites
¼ teaspoon salt
2 ½ Tablespoons water

½ teaspoon cream of tartar
½ cup sugar

In bowl, combine egg whites, salt, and water, and beat until frothy. Add cream of tartar and beat stiff; beat in sugar. Mound meringue on pie, sealing edges to pastry. Serves eight.

THE HAPPY HOUSE
Mayfield

In 1816, GENERAL ANdrew Jackson and governor Isaac Shelby of Kentucky were commissioned by the United States Government to treat with the Chickasaw Indian Nation for a tract of land. After two years of negotiation, they were successful, and "The Jackson Purchase," including all land between the Tennessee and Mississippi rivers, from the Ohio River to the northern Boundary of Mississippi, was added to the states of Kentucky and Tennessee.

Eight counties in southwestern Kentucky came out of the purchase, and settlement began as soon as the Indians migrated to Mississippi.

Near the center of the Kentucky segment of The Purchase is Mayfield, county seat of Graves County, and sometimes called the "Hub of the Purchase." It was settled in 1819 by John Anderson, and was first peopled by Carolinians, later by those who flatboated down the Ohio to Paducah, then traveled overland.

Mayfield has produced many enterprising citizens—an example is Howard D. Happy, known in Mayfield as "the only man who started a business without borrowing a dime."

Happy, a brilliant student, was equipped to become an attorney in 1914 at the age of 19, but was too young to take the bar. Working as a court reporter, he was hired by Royal Typewriter as a field representative in Western Kentucky and Tennessee; he sold his first consignment of three typewriters, and was sent five; he sold those, and was a dealer by 1916. Adding other business machines to his stock, he became the largest office equipment dealer in Western Kentucky, with branches in Paducah and Hopkinsville.

His home, a two-story colonial revival in native brown stone, was designed for gracious living by his wife, and continues the tradition of elegant entertaining as The Happy House Restaurant. Opened in February of 1985 by Pauline Russelberg, The Happy House is decorated in warm rose, ivory, and blue, each room with its own bright, fresh atmosphere, and provides food that is delicious, satisfying, and attractive. "I want it to look like a corsage when it comes out of the kitchen," Pauline said. "It should look pretty as well as taste good."

Lunch choices bear this out, with homemade soups, crisp salads (one combination is spinach, mushrooms, oranges and bacon!) unusual sandwiches, and two quiches a day. For dinner, there are steaks, prime rib, seafood and chicken entrees, with vegetables such as glazed spiced carrots with green grapes. All breads, salad dressings, and desserts are homemade. Especially memorable are Frozen Strawberry Parfait, chess and fudge pies, and rich, fudgy, well-named Miracle Pie.

The Happy House, P.O. Box 52, Mayfield, Kentucky 42066, is at 236 North 8th Street, and is open for lunch Tuesday through Saturday, from 11 a.m. to 2 p.m., and for dinner on Friday and Saturday from 6 to 10 p.m. (502)247-5743. Dress is casual, and no charge cards are accepted; reservations are not necessary, but are preferred for groups of six or more. ($$)

HAPPY HOUSE ASPARAGUS SALAD CUPS

1 pound fresh asparagus
  spears
1 head iceburg lettuce
6 slices bacon, cooked and
  crumbled

⅓ cup sliced ripe olives
8 ounces creamy cucumber
  dressing

Snap off tough ends of asparagus spears. Remove scales from stalks with vegetable peeler, if desired. Cook asparagus, covered, in boiling salted water 6 to 8 minutes or until crisp-tender; drain and chill.

Remove 6 to 8 outer leaves from lettuce, and place on individual serving plates. Shred remaining lettuce; fill lettuce cups with shredded lettuce.

Arrange asparagus spears over shredded lettuce. Sprinkle with bacon and olives. Drizzle dressing over each salad cup. Serves six to eight.

HAPPY HOUSE PRIME RIB QUICHE

One 9-inch deep-dish
  unbaked pie shell
½ cup Parmesan cheese,
  grated
1 cup cooked, chopped
  prime rib meat

½ cup chopped green
  onion
2 cups half and half cream
1 Tablespoon flour
Pinch of paprika
5 eggs, well beaten

Place cheese, meat, and green onion in pie shell. In mixing bowl, combine cream, flour, paprika, and eggs. Pour over other ingredients in shell, and bake at 375 degrees for 45 minutes or until golden brown. Serves eight.

HAPPY HOUSE OATMEAL CORNBREAD

1 cup oatmeal
1 cup self-rising white
  cornmeal
1 cup milk

2 tablespoons bacon
  drippings
2 eggs

In mixing bowl, combine all ingredients. Pour into greased skillet dusted with cornmeal, and bake at 400 degrees for 25 minutes or until brown.

HAPPY HOUSE FANCY GOURMET
CORN STICKS

1 ½ cups self-rising white
corn meal
½ cup self-rising flour
2 Tablespoons sugar

2 eggs
1 cup milk
½ cup bacon drippings
½ cup chopped pecans

In mixing bowl, blend all ingredients well. Spoon into greased cornstick pan, and bake at 400 degrees for about 20 minutes. Yields about two dozen.

INDEX TO RESTAURANTS

INDEX TO RECIPES

Ham and Asparagus Rolls, Whistle Stop, 152
Ham Spread, Holly Hill Inn, 84
Sausage Soufflé, Old Talbott Tavern, 137
Sautéed Sausage and Grits, Ninth Street House, 185

Poultry

Brunswick Stew, Beaumont Inn, 77
California Chicken Salad, Mariah's, 161
Chicken and Dumplings, Iron Kettle, 181
Chicken and Ham au Gratin, Carrollton Inn, 105
Chicken and Fruits Fiesta, Mariah's, 160
Chicken Cordon Bleu, La Taberna, 140
Chicken Martinelli, Dee Felice Café, 41
Chicken Oscar, High Court Inn, 24
Chicken Pot Pie, Barney's Callas Grill, 168
Chicken Salad, Unicorn Tea Room, 100
Chicken Sicilian, Yesterday's, 189
Chicken, Southern Fried, Doe Run Inn, 149
Chicken Tetrazzini, Yesterday's, 188
Crème de Volaille, Duncan Tavern, 28
Hawaiian Chicken Salad, deShā's, 49
Talbott Tavern Gourmet (Chicken breast and country ham), 136

Salads and Dressings

Asparagus Salad Cups, Happy House, 200
Bleu Cheese Dressing, Cunningham's, 121
Blue Cheese Dressing, Bauer's, 117
California Chicken Salad, Mariah's, 161
Chicken Salad, Unicorn Tea Room, 100
Cole Slaw, Iron Kettle, 180
Congealed Spinach Salad with Crabmeat Dressing, Ninth Street House, 184
Cucumber Dressing, Merrick Inn, 60
Cucumber Mousse, Science Hill Inn, 88
French Dressing, Jeremiah's, 196
Frozen Fruit Salad, Beaumont Inn, 76
Fruit Salad, Brodrick's Tavern, 21
Fruit Salad, Barney's Callas Grill, 168
Hawaiian Chicken Salad, deShā's, 49
House Dressing, C. C. Cohen, 193
House Dressing, High Court Inn, 24
House Dressing, Yesterday's, 188
Kentucky Bibb Lettuce with Hot Bacon Dressing, Whistle Stop, 152
Mandarin Orange Salad, Academy Inn, 68
Molded Gazpacho Salad with Creamy Dressing, Holly Hill Inn, 85

Poppy Seed Dressing, John E's, 112
Sauerkraut Salad, Doe Run Inn, 148
Tea Garden Salad and Dressing, Boone Tavern, 32
Thousand Island Dressing, Academy Inn, 69
Thousand Island Dressing, Cunningham's, 121
Three Bean Salad, Doe Run Inn, 148

Sandwiches

Bruddy Curran Sandwich, Bauer's, 116
Hot Brown Sandwich, Brown Hotel, 132
Mike Fink Sandwich, Mike Fink, 37

Seafoods and Fresh Water Fish

Baked Gulf Oysters Cohen, C. C. Cohen, 192
Clam Chowder, Carrollton Inn, 104
Congealed Spinach Salad with Crabmeat Dressing, Ninth Street House, 184
Crab Cakes, Merrick Inn, 61
Halibut Natchez, Mike Fink, 36
Lobster Bar Harbor, Sixth Avenue, 124
Mussels Gino, Dee Felice Café, 40
New Orleans Clam Chowder, Dee Felice Café, 41
Pike with Walnut Butter, Mansion at Griffin Gate, 64
Salmon with Shrimp and Cucumber, Seelbach Hotel, 129
Sautéed Seafood Supreme, Mike Fink, 37
Scalloped Oysters, Brodrick's Tavern, 20
Scallops Jambalaya, C. C. Cohen, 192
Seafood Gumbo, Yesterday's, 189
Shrimp and Scallops Alfredo, Mariah's, 161
Shrimp in Cream and Green Peppercorns, Seelbach Hotel, 128
Stuffed Sole, Dee Felice Café, 40
Turtle Soup, Cunningham's, 120

Soups

Broccoli and Cheese Soup, Mariah's, 160
Broccoli Soup, Unicorn Tea Room, 100
Chicken Velvet soup, Bartholomew's, 172
Chili, deShā's, 48
Clam Chowder, Carrollton Inn, 104
Cream of Cabbage Soup, Science Hill Inn, 88
Creamy Chicken Noodle Soup, Robin's Nest, 108
Dusty's Red Mushroom Soup, Ninth Street House, 185
Loaded Potato Soup, Bartholomew's, 172

New Orleans Clam Chowder, Dee Felice
  Café, 41
Old Fashioned Bean Soup, Old Stable,
  144
Popcorn Soup, Shaker Village, 73
Seafood Gumbo, Yesterday's, 189
Split Pea Soup, John E's, 112
Turtle Soup, Cunningham's, 120

Veal

Lemon Veal, Dudley's, 52
Veal Parmesan, Trattoria Mattei, 96
Veal Patrizzia, Casa Executiva, 56

Vegetables

Artichoke and Spinach Casserole, Elmwood Inn, 80
Cabbage Pudding, Depot, 16

Carrot or Asparagus Soufflé, Beaumont
  Inn, 77
Corn Pudding, Old Stable, 144
French Fried Eggplant, Skyline Supper
  Club, 176
Hearts of Artichokes Fondue, Boone Tav-
  ern, 33
Potato Pancakes, Mick Noll's, 45
Scalloped Eggplant, Barney's Callas
  Grill, 169
Scalloped Zucchini, Old Stone Inn, 92
Seasoned Green Beans, Old Stable, 144
Spinach Casserole, Cunningham's, 121
Squash Casserole, Merrick Inn, 60
Stuffed Eggplant, Old Stone Inn, 93
Stuffed Potatoes Bauer's, 116
Summer Squash Casserole, Elmwood
  Inn, 81
Vegetable Pie, The Robin's Nest, 108